Seducing Spirits
and Doctrines
of Demons

Seducing Spirits and Doctrines of Demons

Rick Renner

Albury Publishing
Tulsa, Oklahoma

Unless otherwise noted, all Scripture quotations are from the *King James Version* of the Bible.

6th Printing
Over 46,000 in Print

Seducing Spirits and Doctrines of Demons

ISBN 1-88008-907-6

Published by Albury Publishing
P. O. Box 740406
Tulsa, Oklahoma 74147-0406

Dedication

To my beloved and precious wife and sister in the Lord, Denise.

Contents

Foreword

Rick Renner preached this series at Grace Fellowship. I am pleased to see it being published in a book. It was one of the most timely messages I have heard, and it has impacted many of my sermons since.

Seducing Spirits and Doctrines of Demons is an accurate insight from Paul's letter to Timothy of the day we are living in. Rick paints a clear picture of Satan at work in the world today in the New Age Movement, imitating the role of the Church.

He also tells of Satan's attack in the Church itself to lure believers away from the foundation of the Word of God and chase only after miracles and the supernatural.

Rick brings a balanced truth to those who long to hear the Word of Truth rightly divided. It is a pleasure to recommend Rick Renner as an able minister and my friend.

Bob Yandian, Pastor
Grace Fellowship
Tulsa, Oklahoma

Chapter 1
Last-Day Supernatural Confrontation

Recently the New Age Movement has been gaining widespread popularity. With all of its glamour, sponsorship by celebrities, and supernatural activities, it is alluring millions into its web of deception. There, caught in a demonic seduction, Satan is conspiring to attack and victimize the world — inoculating the world with a deadly serum — a serum that will eventually mesmerize the world over with supernatural phenomena unrelated to God.

This tragedy is far worse than we could ever state. There is a worldwide seduction taking place now, and we, as the Church, must know how to respond. The Church is not unaffected by these seducing spirits and doctrines of demons.

Another satanic seduction is taking place. This one is by far more serious, for it is a seduction occurring right in the midst of the Church. Some, because of a God-given hunger for the supernatural, are intruding into realms of the Spirit without the assistance of God. It looks right, and it sounds spiritual, but there is a hook in these new teachings that eventually could hurt the Church and throw it off into error as damaging as that of the New Age Movement.

It is time to stand up and shout the truth about this potential danger. A great delusion is taking place! It is time for us to come before God in all honesty — confessing our lack of power, lack of revival, and lack of God-given

1

visitations. Then we will be in a position to receive the real move of God's Spirit we all desire.

The New Age or the Last Days?

Second Timothy chapter 3 deals with "last days" occurrences. As we study this powerful section of scripture, we will deal with these current errors in the world and in the Church. Second Timothy chapter 3 reads and sounds very much like a current issue of your newspaper or tonight's national news program. While Satan is proclaiming this to be the New Age, never before has it been more evident that this is the Last Age, as we have known mankind.

Tremendous changes — in financial systems, political systems, nature and, of course, religious systems — are now taking place. We must have a clear understanding of what the scripture teaches about these last very difficult days and how we must respond to them.

The Church is now headed for its greatest hour! God is waiting for us to come before the cross, empty ourselves before Him, and yield to the strongest move of God's power that the earth has ever seen! Regardless of the scandals of recent years, the Church is going to rise to break new ground and take dominion as never before! We are headed for a confrontation of supernatural powers — and God is going to reveal just how powerful He really is!

Perilous Times Shall Come

Turn in your Bible to Second Timothy chapter 3:

This know also, that in the last days perilous times shall come.

For men shall be lovers of their own selves, covetous, boasters, proud, blasphemers, disobedient to parents, unthankful, unholy.

Without natural affection, trucebreakers, false accusers, incontinent, fierce, despisers of those that are good,

2

Traitors heady, high-minded, lovers of pleasures more than lovers of God;

Having a form of godliness, but denying the power thereof: from such turn away.

For of this sort are they which creep into houses, and lead captive silly women laden with sins, led away with divers lusts.

Ever learning, and never able to come to the knowledge of the truth.

Now as Jannes and Jambres withstood Moses, so do these also resist the truth: men of corrupt minds, reprobate concerning the faith.

But they shall proceed no further, for their folly shall be manifest unto all men, as theirs also was.

2 Timothy 3:1-9

Skip down to verse 13, where Paul says, "But evil men and seducers shall wax worse and worse, deceiving, and being deceived." This is a very important verse. In the Greek, where Paul says, "they shall wax worse and worse," this is in the comparative tense. And when Timothy read it, what it meant was this: "Timothy, you think men are evil now, but it is going to be far, far, far worse at the end of the age."

In fact, the Greek language actually means that these men shall suddenly gain a rate of speed that is alarming. They've been with us for a while, but all of a sudden they will pick up speed and immediately cut through to the worse stage, having an impact upon the entire globe. They shall cut through to the worst stage, deceiving and being deceived.

This word "seducers" is actually the Greek word for sorcerers! The last days will experience the worst of all evils — including a revival of sophisticated sorcery.

Problems in the World's System

The things we see in Second Timothy chapter 3 should not be problems on the inside of the Church. These are problems that belong to the world's system. If these are

3

problems of the world, why does Paul write to Timothy about them? Because Church members don't live within the walls of the Church 24 hours a day, seven days a week. They live their life in the world. They go out into the world. They come back into the Church.

And the reason Paul is so specific in chapter 3 is he knows unless the people are warned, they will pick up the attitude of the world, carry the attitude of the world back into the Church, and then the problems within the Church will be greater than they already are. So Paul says, "Son, let me tell you about the world. You alarm your people to the facts."

Look at chapter 3 verse 1 and see what he says. "This know also, that in the last days perilous times shall come." I want you to notice several words: the word "know," the word "last," the word "perilous," and the word "times." These are very important words.

First of all, in verse 1, Paul says "This know also." This word "know" is the Greek word *ginosko*. It would be better translated, "Realize these facts. Come to recognize what is happening." And by selecting this word, the Holy Ghost is telling us some of these things cannot be changed; not even by prayer. A better translation really would be, "Come to grips with these certain facts which cannot be changed."

This tells Timothy, "Timothy, this is going to happen in the world, whether you like it or not. There's nothing you can do to stop it. Therefore, come to accept it. Come to recognize it. Come to grips with these alarming facts."

The Last of the Last Days

Notice the next phrase: "in the last days perilous times shall come." This phrase "last days" is from the Greek word *eschatos*, which unmistakably means "the *last* of the last days." This is where we get the word *eschatology*, which is the study of last days. So we're talking about things that happen just prior to the coming of the Lord.

4

And notice how Paul describes these days. He says they are "perilous times." But what does the word "perilous" mean? This is the Greek word *chalepos*. Understand what the word *chalepos* really means. In the Bible it is translated "perilous," but the word *chalepos* actually is the word "treacherous." Treacherous times shall come. You could translate it, "difficult times shall come." A fine translation would be, "dangerous times shall come."

Really, the whole idea of this word "perilous," the word *chalepos*, can be translated again, "treacherous, dangerous, difficult, hard." The idea is "a high-risk period." The whole period is encumbered with risk, danger, harm, hurt. And Paul says the last of the last days will be like that.

What is interesting is the next word: "times." This is the Greek word *kairos*. This word *kairos* refers to specific, allotted periods of time, like centuries, or like millenniums. But right here the idea is decades. It would be fine to translate it, "In the last of the last days difficult decades will come. And each new decade will add its own measure of new danger, new risk, new harm, and new hurt."

I don't know about you, but I think that's a perfect description of this century, because every decade of this century has provided new thinking, new psychologies which basically have eroded respect, have eroded authority, and have eroded man's belief in God. It's taken prayer out of the schools. Now they're trying to take "in God we trust" off the money. You can go on down the line. There's an attack on the churches now.

Each decade during this century seems to have added its own special kind of harm and special hurt. Second Timothy 3 verse 1 says that's exactly what would happen. I think that makes this verse very up-to-date.

Decades of Hurt

Here is the idea: Each decade will add its measure of hurt. The twenties will add its measure of hurt. The thirties will add its new measure of thinking. The forties, the fifties, the sixties, the seventies — all of these different allotted periods of time are working together, adding to the next and to the next and to the next and to the next.

And they are working, working, working, and culminating eventually to produce a world that is a very dangerous place to live in. It is a high-risk place. It's a place that has great hurts and great harms. And if you live in it, you'll be hurt by it. It's decades upon decades — working, working, and working to produce a world that is dangerous. What we're talking about is the mystery of lawlessness.

Then at the beginning of verse 2, the Holy Spirit gives us a clue to these perilous times and what the primary characteristics of those perilous times will be. You will never get it if you have a *King James Version*. In fact, you may not get it if you have a *New International Version*. You probably won't get it unless you have a Greek Bible.

Look in verse 2. It says, "For men shall be. . . ." Notice those two words, "shall be." This phrase "shall be" is the future tense of the word *eimi*. Now pay attention carefully to this clue which the Holy Spirit is giving us in scripture. This word *eimi*, "shall be," is the Greek word literally translated "I am." The word *eimi* in verse 2 leaves the ideas of self-centeredness, selfishness, or a generation of people who are "I am." They look out for *themselves* before anyone else. They have an inordinate preoccupation with *themselves*.

'The Me Generation'

This is a generation of people who are self-centered and self-seeking. They are selfish. They are the "I am" generation. That would describe this generation, the day in which we live, better than any other day there has ever been before now. This is the day of *I am. I am.* Secular Humanism is the worship of the deity of man. Man is arriving. Man is becoming. This is the day when man is saying, "I am."

6

Then, to make sure we understand, Paul says "For men shall be lovers of their own selves. . . ." That is a strange phrase, because the Greek word here is the Greek word *philautos*, from *philos*, which means to love, or have love for a friend. The word *autos* is where we get the word for autobiography. The word *autos* means "myself." So we're talking about love for one's self. But here it's talking about something that is abnormal or inordinate. It's good to respect yourself — it's good to take care of yourself — but this is talking about something that's not normal. This is an inordinate preoccupation with yourself.

The Bible says that this will be the primary major characteristic of the last days. Men will be "I am," developing an inordinate passion for themselves, engrossed with themselves and in love with themselves — more committed to themselves than to anyone else, because this is the "I am" generation.

This is nowhere more evident than at the magazine rack of the grocery store. Have you ever noticed the names of the magazines? We're talking about a generation of people who are preoccupied with themselves. *Muscle and Fitness. Flex. Runner. Fisher. Jogger.* One magazine is called *Self. New Woman.* If you don't believe me, go and look.

We have become a society that is totally hedonistic. We are passionately working to develop ourselves and cater to our own creature comforts. We have abandoned everything else for the sake of self.

Selfishness in the Church

This spirit of selfishness and self-centeredness today is not only in the world. It has found its way into the Church, but it is disguised inside the Church. We have garbed it in spiritual terms. Let me tell you the first place where it manifests: when the nursery needs workers! Do you know what people say? "I'll miss the service." "I can't go back there because *I*. . ." "Well, I would, but *I*." "*I*."

I remember when I was growing up in the Southern Baptist Church. I might knock the Baptist Church, but I wouldn't trade my background for any other, because I was taught servanthood in the Baptist Church.

I was taught in the Baptist Church that it was a joy to serve the Lord. You wouldn't even think about being paid to serve the Lord. It was a joy. It was a privilege. It was an honor to serve the Lord. Now the spirit of the world has gotten into the Church, and everyone is out to take care of himself. "Well now, I'll do it, but will it eventually work into a full-time position?"

Look in verse 2 and see what it says next. "For men shall be lovers of their own selves, covetous...." Underline the word "covetous," because this word "covetous" is the very first *result* of someone who is inordinately in love with himself. This word "covetous" is the Greek word *philarguros*, which refers to an abnormal love for money.

If you love yourself more than anything else in the world, what do you need to make your life comfortable? You need money. And, really, the whole idea of the word "covetous" is an inordinate passion for materialism. If you're looking out for number one, you're self-centered, and your whole world revolves around you, you will scrap everything else in order to provide your own comforts. I want you to see that these two things are associated one with the other.

Look at the next word. The next word says, "boasters." The word "boasters" is the Greek word *alazon*, which means "to boast, to brag, to exaggerate to the point of lying, in order that you might make an advance and make a gain of someone else." Again, this is the "I am" generation. They are so concerned about themselves that morals no longer count; standards no longer matter.

Situational Ethics Popular

Situational Ethics are the very best standard for this kind of a generation. "Whatever is best for me right now, that's what I'm going to do." This will be a characteristic of the last days: a people who throw out standards. If they can advance themselves, if they can make a gain, if they can make more money — fine. They'll do anything, they'll say anything, they'll exaggerate, they'll boast, they'll brag, even to the point of lying, with no conviction about doing it.

Then the scripture says, "proud." The word "proud" describes a spirit of superiority. This word "proud" really is the word "superiority," which describes the mentality of the man who thinks he's better than everyone else in the world. As a result of this, these people become "blasphemers."

If you think you're better than anyone else, suddenly you are in a position to judge everyone else. And this describes a generation of people who are haughty, arrogant, and superior. They have an opinion about everything.

When you throw morals out and you create your own morals, you are making yourself into God! You say, "Well, I know what's right for my life. Don't tell me what the Bible says, because I know what's right. The Bible is just one way. I have my own way." You then place yourself on your own level of spirituality, and from that position you are able to judge everyone else.

Out With the Standards

There's no place where this is more evident than the movies. People have thrown out ethics, holiness, standards, fidelity — they've thrown it *all* out! And they have become blasphemous. They have become abusive. This word "blasphemy" actually refers to something that is violent.

I'm just speaking generally. There are some good movies; I know that. I like to go to the show. But what they're saying on the motion picture screen today wasn't said when I was a little boy! And they don't say it once or twice in a movie. Very freely, they say whatever they want.

They have no standard that says that is wrong. They've thrown the standard out. Their only standard is: "I'm going to do what I want to do — what will profit me the most — and what's going to make me the most comfortable." That is their standard.

Children Out of Control

Notice what it says next: "disobedient to parents." That phrase "disobedient to parents" is the Greek word *apeithos*. This is what this word *apeithos* means. *Peithos* is the Greek word which means "to be persuadable." But if you put a privitive on the front of it, it's a-peithos, and it means children who are *un*persuadable, or *un*controllable.

If you talk to them and try to control them, it's almost as though the children are unable to hear! You are unable to control them. Regardless of how much you do, you cannot persuade them. You've lost control of them. They're children running wild — children beyond control — children who are unpersuadable. This is definitely a characteristic of the day in which we live!

Twenty years ago, our problems in school were cheating, tardiness, and talking in class. Now our schools have security guards in elementary as well as junior high and high schools, checking the kids for guns, knives, and drugs. Our children used to smoke cigarettes in the bathroom. Today they're putting needles in their arms and free-basing cocaine.

Because the Word has been thrown out of many homes, and it is no longer regarded, sexual purity has become a thing of the past. The influence of television, rock 'n' roll, and movies has created an image that tells today's youth, "Do whatever you want to do!"

Then, when the AIDS crisis should have awakened our world to this deep, deep moral deterioration, instead, condoms are given to *the kids!*

It is no small wonder that children are unpersuadable and beyond control!

Chapter 2
Unthankful and Unholy

Notice the next statement here in Second Timothy 3:2: "unthankful and unholy." These things always go together: unthankful and unholy. Where there is unthankfulness, there is always unholiness. This word "unthankful" is a word which refers to a thanksgiving to God.

The Bible says that in the *last* of the last days, the world will be a place where thanksgiving has ceased to flow. Here is the thing about thanksgiving: If you are thankful, that means you are looking to someone to give thanks.

But this is the generation that has dammed up thanksgiving. They have purposefully shut it off. And, really, this word "thanksgiving" is a Greek word, *charistos*, which refers to something that freely flows. It's where we get the word "grace." However, here it is the word *acharistos*, which means the condition has been reversed — the thanksgiving has been dammed up — it's no longer flowing.

And it isn't that these people are ignorant of God. It's that they no longer want to thank God. They no longer desire to recognize Him. So they moved, rather, from thankfulness to unthankfulness.

They have decided to reject God — to ignore Him — to stop pursuing Him and being thankful to Him. And where you cease to look to God, you begin to look to yourself. And the result of this is what? *Unholiness.*

11

The word "unholy" is the Greek word *anosios*, which refers to something that is "lewd, nasty, or dirty." I don't know about you, but that's another good description, I think, of the culture that we live in today. It's lewd, it's nasty, and it's dirty! Moral filth is today the main subject matter of comedians. Lewd, nasty, and dirty — who would have ever believed twenty years ago that this type of talk and behavior would be comical?

I can guarantee from scripture that where people are unthankful, they become unholy. If thankfulness has ceased to flow out of your heart, you're headed for a life that is not holy. The next step is unholiness.

A Lost World

Thankfulness is an indicator of where you are spiritually. If you're not thankful, you're in trouble, because you're headed for unholiness. Look at Romans 1. I want you to see what it says in verse 21. It's talking about a lost world. It says, "Because that, when they knew God, they glorified him not as God, and neither were" — what? — "thankful...."

Unthankfulness or ingratitude is the first major step to moral deterioration. That is what the Bible is saying here, because they glorified Him not as God, neither were thankful. They ceased to look to God. They ceased to glorify Him. They ceased to pursue Him.

The Bible says, "...but became vain in their imaginations." And this word "vain" is a Greek word, *mataios*, which means "they were wasted in their imaginations." And this word "imaginations" is a Greek word for reasoning or thought processes.

The way that they think suddenly became messed up. The way that they reasoned suddenly became infiltrated by wrong reasoning. They were wasted in their intelligence. They began to make deductions intellectually that don't even make sense. (I think evolution is a great example of this.)

When you cease to be thankful, when you cease to be glorifying God, your imagination is wasted.

Notice what it says next in verse 21: They were wasted in their reasonings, and "their foolish heart was darkened." Now pay attention to the word "heart." What does it say was on the inside of their foolish heart? *Darkness.* Their foolish heart was darkened. This word "heart" is a Greek word, *kardia.*

Hearts Pumping Darkness

If you want to know how bad the world is going to be, this word *kardia* tells us, because it says their foolish heart was darkened. What does the heart do? It pumps blood. Blood goes into every part of the body. There's not a part of your body that is not touched by blood. Only this heart, mentioned in verse 21, does not have blood in it. This heart has *darkness* in it.

The whole idea is, when they ceased to glorify God and turned to themselves, their intelligence was wasted. They ceased to even know God, and their heart became darkened and began to pump and pump darkness. And just like the human heart pumps blood into every part of the human body, this spiritually darkened heart will pump darkness throughout all humanity.

Have you ever noticed how today they are creating evil things that we've never even heard of before? It's because their foolish heart is pumping darkness.

I'll tell you what's exciting, Church: Ephesians 1:18 says, "The eyes of your understanding being enlightened. . . ." In Greek the word "understanding" is the same Greek word *kardia,* or "heart."

Just as the heart pumps blood for the body, the Church should have light in its heart. And like the heart pumps blood, in the Church, our hearts should be pumping light, light, and more light.

We should see more, know more, and understand more than we ever have, because our hearts have been enlightened. They are full of illumination and revelation, and they are pumping the glory of God in us and in the Church. But the heart of the world is pumping darkness. Their foolish heart has become darkened.

Look at the next verse, Romans 1:22. "Professing themselves to be wise, they became fools." The word "fools" is the Greek word *moraino.* What word do we get from that? "Moron." They became morons! Have you noticed that the "wiser" and more "sophisticated" we claim to be, the more "moronic" our society is becoming? There is no real wisdom without God. The Bible says, "They became morons."

And notice in verse 23 what the morons did: The morons "changed the glory of the uncorruptible God into an image made like to corruptible man, and to birds, and four-footed beasts, and creeping things." In verse 23, the word "changed" is really the word "exchange." They exchanged the glory of God. Really, it's the very Greek word which means "I think I found a better bargain, and therefore I'll make a trade."

A Bad Bargain

They thought man was a better bargain than God. So rather than worshipping God, they made an exchange; they made a bargain for what they thought was a better deal. And this is why the Bible says they were morons. They thought this was a better bargain than God. And it says, "They changed the glory of the uncorruptible God into an image made like to corruptible man, and to birds, and four-footed beasts, and creeping things."

If I were you, I would circle that entire verse in your Bible. And please take a note of this, because the Holy Spirit here is giving us another clue. What you find in verse 23 is the history of mankind in a backward report.

14

Paul begins with where we are *now*. He says, "Today we worship corruptible *man*. But before that, we were more primitive, and we worshipped *birds*. Before that, we worshipped four-footed *beasts*. And before that, we worshipped *creeping things*." So he's describing the history of mankind.

And if you study, history will bear it out: Man originally worshipped creeping things, then four-footed beasts, then birds, and now we've moved beyond the animal kingdom, and today who do we worship? We worship man.

This is what the doctrine of Secular Humanism is. And if you read the Secular Humanist Manifesto, it says there is no supernatural God to intervene in the affairs of man. There is only man. And it is that teaching today which is working in our school system. It's working in culture. It's working in the arts. It's working on the television. It's coming to us from every angle.

Secular Humanism and the Fall of Greece

What is the ultimate end of Secular Humanism? Is it the perfection of man, as they claim? Do you know what it is? *A society that begins to take on homosexual characteristics!*

You say, "Now, Rick, what are you saying?" I'm saying that if you worship man, God will give you the desire of your heart. That's exactly what Romans 1 says. Study history. Study the Greeks.

What did the Greeks have standing on every corner? Statues of who? Man. Art forms. Oh, they worshipped the male anatomy. They worshipped the female anatomy. Oh, man, man, man. And they had philosophers. They had scientists. They had inventors. They were the "I am" generation of their day. And what eventually happened to the society of Greece? It became morally ruined.

I have spent a great deal of time studying Greek history. It was popular right before the destruction of Greek culture to be bisexual. In fact, if you were just a heterosexual, they'd

15

say you were primitive, you were closed-minded, and you were far behind everyone else.

"The human body is so beautiful. It is so beautiful the way man has developed. Therefore, since it's so beautiful, it's fine to mingle yourself together with it, regardless of what concoction it comes in." That was the thought of Greek culture. That was the thought of Roman culture. And today it's happening in the United States!

Some say, "We didn't hear about homosexual parades a few years ago, and we didn't hear as much about homosexuality then as we hear about it today." Other people say, "Well, they've just come out of the closet now." No, no, no, no!

When you leave the Bible and you leave standards; when you leave the ethics of the Word and you scrap all those beliefs in order to make up your own; and when you enter into the worship of man, *anything* is game. And that is exactly what we find in Romans chapter 1.

We need a Holy Ghost revival. Do you know what else we need: We need the strong teaching of the Word to set us straight on these issues; especially during these days when the world is bombarding us from every direction.

The World Seeps into the Church

Some of you are affected by the thinking of the world, and you don't even know it. The thinking of the world includes books that basically say, "None of us need help from God, because we're all O.K." That's basically what the philosophy of the world today is: self. There's no mention of God. In fact, anything religious or spiritual, as speaking from the Word of God, would be laughed at. You see, these things are slowly working their way into the mainstream of the world. And the world at large is buying into this philosophy.

That's why Paul said to Timothy, "You'd better come to grips with these facts, and you'd better tell your church about it so this problem does not get inside your church."

Look at Romans 1 verse 24. I don't know about you, but I think this is important information. Verse 24 says, "Wherefore God gave them up to uncleanness through the lusts of their own hearts, to dishonour their own bodies between themselves."

This verse is greatly misunderstood. People say, "Well, that's not fair. God just gave them up!" That's not what it says. It says, "God gave them up to the" — what? — "lusts of their own hearts." Since they had mankind in their heart, and they wanted to worship man, God gave them what they wanted.

God's a good God. He will let you worship anything you want to worship. However, whatever you worship, you'll want to become "one" with. If you worship God, you'll want to be "one" with God. If you worship Jesus, you'll want to be "one" with Jesus. And in time, if you worship man, you'll want to become "one" with man.

In this verse where it says, "God gave them up," the whole idea is, "God released them." His attitude was, "Fine, if that's what you want, go get it. If you want to worship man — if that's the lust that's in your heart — go get it." And God knew what the result would be.

Exchanging Truth for a Lie

Notice what it says. "To dishonour their own bodies between themselves: Who changed the truth of God into a lie. . . ." Notice the word "change." Again, it's the Greek word which means they "exchanged." They knew what the truth was. The truth was available. They could read it. They could listen to it. But they no longer wanted the truth.

They made a bargain for something they thought was better. They made a deal. They made a trade. They knew the truth, and they traded it in and took something else. They exchanged the truth of God into a lie. "And worshipped and served" — who? *The creature.* That's man. ". . . and

17

worshipped and served the creature more than the Creator, who is blessed for ever, Amen" (v. 25).

Look at the next verses. "For this cause God gave them up unto vile affections; for even their women did change the natural use into that which is against nature: And likewise also the men, leaving the natural use of the woman, burned in their lust one toward another; men with men working that which is unseemly, and receiving in themselves that recompence of their error which was meet. And even as they did not like to retain God..." (vv. 26-28). Pay heed to the phrase "did not like." It wasn't that they didn't know the truth, or they didn't know God. They no longer wanted to hear God.

Dirt Falling on Their Coffin

That's exactly what's happening in our world today. They're saying, "You Bible-thumpers, get out of here! Don't preach at us. We don't want to hear it." The mass media are lambasting the Church, saying we're Holy Joes and we don't know anything. Why? Because we raise a standard of the Word. And every time we preach the Word, it's like clods of dirt falling on their coffin, and they know the judgment of God is nigh.

That's why Romans 1:18 says, "For the wrath of God is revealed from heaven against all ungodliness and unrighteousness of men, who hold the truth in unrighteousness." The word "hold" is the Greek word *katecho*. It means "to have something in hand and to hold it down," or "to suppress it." It's not that they don't know it. They are suppressing it.

People know the truth. They may not want to deal with it. They may try to suppress it. They may try to get it off the air, get it off the radio, get it out of sight, thinking, "Out of sight, out of mind. Let's suppress it. Let's push it down. Let's try to destroy it. If it's out of sight, it's out of mind.

Then we will no longer be convicted by it." And that is why verse 28 says, "They did not like to retain God."

Notice this: "And even as they did not like to retain God in their knowledge, God gave them over to a reprobate mind." I want you to know, God will give you over to what you want!

"God gave them over to a reprobate mind, to do those things which are not convenient; Being filled with all unrighteousness, fornication, wickedness, covetousness, maliciousness; full of envy, murder, debate, deceit, malignity; whisperers, Backbiters, haters of God, despiteful, proud, boasters, inventors of evil things, disobedient to parents" (vv. 28-30).

Do you know what we are reading? We are reading the fruit of Secular Humanism — this is exactly what we are reading. The worship of man and self-deification produces all of these things, because there is no standard. A Secular Humanist philosophy says, "I am God; therefore, I can judge myself and do what I want to do."

There's Hope for Homosexuals

I want to say something to you if you're bound in the sin of homosexuality. God is not against you. He's not. God is for you. I don't have anything against you: not one, not one at all.

I want to tell you why you are the way you are. Number one, the devil had a plan to destroy your life. Number two, you were born in a dangerous, harmful, hurtful time, when the psychologies of man are telling us there are alternate lifestyles.

The authority of the Bible has been eroded; therefore, it no longer has authority in society. It is producing this world situation, and you are a by-product of it. You're not a by-product of your parents. You're a by-product of a civilization that has gone astray. And I want you to know that you, like the world, are a victim, and Jesus Christ can set you free!

Go back to where we started, over in Second Timothy chapter 3. I want you to see what it says: "Unthankful, unholy." Remember, everything we saw in Romans chapter 1 began because a society refused to glorify God and thank Him. And when people cease to thank God, unholiness is always the result — always.

When a society ceases to thank God, ceases to pray to God, ceases to glorify Him, it's going to result in the deification of man, horrible morals, and unholiness. Again, this word "unholy" could be translated, "lewd, filthy, nasty, dirty," and so forth.

Look at verses 3 and 4: "Without natural affection, trucebreakers, false accusers, incontinent, fierce, despisers of those that are good, Traitors heady, highminded, lovers of pleasures more than lovers of God."

Go back to verse 3 and look again at the phrase "without natural affection." Some say that this refers to the sin of homosexuality or lesbianism. Wrong, wrong, wrong! That has already been dealt with in the previous verse.

A Prediction of Divorce

This phrase "without natural affection" literally means "without love for natural family." And this describes a day in which a natural love for your mom and dad begins to dissipate, or family loyalty begins to be a thing of the past. People cease to have the loyalty for their son, for their daughter, for their mother, for their uncle, for their grandmother, that they once had. This means without natural affection, or affection for members of your own family. That's happening today all the time.

Look what it says here: "Without natural affection." Now notice what happens as a result of this: "Trucebreakers." Where there is no love for family, where there is no longer

20

a strong commitment to a husband or a wife, do you know what happens? There is a breaking of a truce.

This word "trucebreaker" is actually the Greek word for "irreconcilable differences." It means, families will be unable to come to grips with one another; they will not be able to reconcile. The idea is, it will be like mass hysteria; an experience that supercedes anything that has ever happened prior to the last days. And this word refers to divorce, trucebreakers, and irreconcilable differences, which immediately result in "false accusers."

Dealing With the Devil

You see, this is a chain of events. Next notice the phrase "false accusers," because this is from the Greek word *diabolos*. Do you know what the Greek word *diabolos* is? That is the word "devil." It's bad enough to be an accuser, but the Bible here uses the word "devil," meaning people are going to become so proficient in the art of slander and in the art of accusing, you're going to think you're dealing with the devil himself!

I watched a "trial" (it wasn't supposed to be a trial, but it was) of Judge Robert Bork, and we were dealing with proficient accusers. It was the *diabolos* in action. The mass media today have sadly fallen into the hands of the *diabolos*. Through the mass media, the devil is accusing everything that has even a hint of righteousness in it.

Notice what it says next: "False accusers, incontinent." You say, "What in the world does 'incontinent' mean?" In one meeting I asked the question, "Do you know what 'incontinent' means?" A nurse responded, "Well, that refers to older people who can't control their bladder."

I don't think this means we're going to have worldwide bladder problems. This word "incontinent" is actually the Greek word for "power" — *akratos* — but it's power that is out of control. And the idea is, in the last of the last days, power is going to go out of control.

21

A World Out of Control

This word "power" would refer to government out of control. It would refer to world financial systems that are completely out of control. They are wacko — off base — running wild. They cannot be controlled. This would be a word used to describe the stock market, credit cards, sex, passion — anything.

The whole idea is, the world basically will be a world that has uncontrollable appetites. They will not know how to say no. That is why the Congress of the United States cannot quit spending money. They do not know how to say no. This is a generation of reckless spenders. Power is out of control.

I will never forget when I went to speak with some politicians, and they told me what was going on in the world system. They told me what would happen in the next two years, and what would happen in the next eight years, and what possibly could happen in the next 16 years.

I just sat in my chair and laughed, because it seems this whole thing is completely out of control. What can we do to help? What can we do to change? When I went to bed that night, I lay there and laughed and laughed and laughed. I felt absolutely helpless. What can you, we, or anyone do?

I was walking around stunned — absolutely stunned — at what they told me was going to happen to the United States, what was going to happen in the White House, and what was going to happen to the world financial markets because the Congress won't say no. It would greatly disturb you if you knew what they told me. It's out of control! We live in a world that is out of control!

Fierce, Untamable, Uncivilized

Look at the next word in verse 3: "fierce." Do you know what this word is? This is the Greek word *anemeros*, which means "untamable." And the idea is, this thing is so far out of control, no one is going to be able to tame it — no one!

And you can write it down — you can be guaranteed of it, based on Scripture — it doesn't matter who is elected President now or in the future; this thing is out of control! It has gone too far. It is on a head-on collision course with disaster. It is out of control. It is untamable.

In fact, this word "fierce," *anemeros,* is actually the word which means "uncivilized." It describes a world that is so untamable that eventually it will become a place where people behave as though they are uncivilized. You say, "Then why even vote now or in the future? Why get involved if things are already too far out of control?" By electing God's man and letting our voice be heard, we may *delay* the inevitable. More time means more souls saved.

And the next statement — oh, you'll get a laugh out of this one — the next statement says, "despisers of those that are good." What does that mean? That is actually a Greek technical word that refers to a country where there are no laws for good people!

Have you ever felt like the law today only protected the bad people? The Bible says this will be an evidence of the last days. Why? Because men have a reprobate mind. Their intelligence has been wasted. "No laws for good people..." Imagine living in a day when it is criminal to *stop* someone from murdering an unborn child. Society thinks it is *advancing!* In reality, it is deteriorating and becoming uncivilized!

Looking for That 'Quick Fix'

Look at verse 4. It says, "traitors." This word "traitors" means "willing to break an oath in order to make a gain." The word "heady" describes the attitude of temporal-minded people. This word "heady" really is the word for "a quick fix."

The idea is, these will be people who do not think in the long term. They just think in the short term. "Well now, I don't care what the long-term results are. What's it going to do for us right now?" They are not people who have enough sense to even think about the long term; the long run of their decision. They don't really care what's going to happen to the next generation. All they care about is what's going to happen to them right now. Therefore, they make reckless, hasty decisions, not thinking things all the way through, in order to make themselves a little more comfortable right now.

Notice what it says next. It says, "highminded." This word "highminded" is the Greek word *tuphoo*, from which we get the word "typhoon." Now you say, "Does this mean we're going to have worldwide typhoons?" No, it means that this last hedonistic society will roll across the earth like a hurricane. It's going to be loud, it's going to be boisterous, it's going to do its best to roll over, blow everything down, and crush every traditional institution in its way.

But just as fast as it came — just that fast — it will crumble. Now I don't know about you, but I'm glad I belong to the kingdom that is unshakable. (I'm getting more grateful with every word we're covering here.)

Look at the next statement. What does it say? "Lovers of pleasures more than lovers of God." This word "pleasure" is the Greek word for hedonistic pleasures. This is a society that delights in excessive luxury and pleasure.

Really, do you know what their philosophy is? "Spend a lot; waste a lot." Hedonistic pleasures. "Spend a lot, live a lot, waste a lot — nothing matters except the moment that we're in right now." And the Greek actually says, "lovers of pleasure more than lovers of God."

Again, the whole idea is, they made an exchange. They know that God is there, but they no longer take God seriously. What is now serious to them is life. It is their suntan. It is a new house that they want. Forget God, forget the Word, forget tithing, forget offerings — forget all of that. What is important is *now*, and what I feel *now*, and what I need *now*. Hedonistic pleasures.

24

Denying God's Power

Look at verse 5. It says, "Having a form of godliness, but denying the power thereof...." Notice it doesn't say they deny power. It says they deny "the power thereof." "Thereof" refers to God's power. The verse continues, "...from such turn away."

You know, if all you had was verse 6, you would think it referred to Jehovah's Witnesses: "For of this sort are they which creep into houses, and lead captive silly women laden with sins, led away with divers lusts."

Then you come to verse 7, and it sounds like a description of Charismatics: "Ever learning, and never able to come to the knowledge of the truth." Who are these verses talking about?

Look at the next two verses. Verses 8 and 9 tell us who these verses are talking about: "Now as Jannes and Jambres withstood Moses, so do these also resist the truth: men of corrupt minds, reprobate concerning the faith. But they shall proceed no further: for their folly shall be manifest unto all men, as theirs also was."

The Occult End-Time Revival

Verses 5 through 9 and verse 13 describe the activity of an end-time revival. But this revival is not a Holy Ghost revival. This is an *occult revival!* So really, verses 5 through 9 and verse 13 describe a revival of the occult in the last days.

It wasn't until recent years that anyone knew what these verses really were describing. We would study these verses and we would think, "Well, maybe it's dead denominations. Maybe it's Jehovah Witnesses. Maybe it's Christian cults."

But the Bible plainly says it is — who? Jannes and Jambres. We're talking about the spirit of Jannes and Jambres. Now who were Jannes and Jambres? The two primary sorcerers who opposed the ministry of Moses. Jannes and Jambres were able to work signs and wonders. They were

25

able to prophesy. They were able to do incredible miracles — miracles spawned by a genuine satanic anointing.

Chapter 3
The Hollow Revival

Fifteen years ago, you could hardly find a book on the devil in the local bookstores. But today, the Executive Director of the New Age Publishing and Retailing Alliance reports there are currently more than 2,500 occult bookstores in the U.S., and well over 3,000 publishers of occult journals and books.

Whereas fifteen years ago, you could hardly find a book on the subject, today occultism is a major, multi-billion-dollar business. Recent estimates reveal that more than $1 billion worth of New Age books sell each year.

Even well-known and very established bookstores such as B. Dalton Bookseller and Waldenbooks have New Age sections in their stores. Do you realize that their New Age sections are normally bigger than the Christian, religious sections? I know, because I have been visiting their bookstores all over the United States. I actually count the titles in both sections to compare and see what is selling the most.

In their New Age sections, they have books on crystals, spirit-writing, spirit-guides and, of course, channeling, which really disturbs me, because the word "channeling" is a new word for "medium." That's all it is. And I'm going to tell you why it disturbs me: They stole that word from the Church!

I grew up in my church singing, "Make me a channel of blessing today. Make me a channel of blessing, I pray."

We're the ones who are supposed to be channels; not the occult. And that is why I like to pray, "Lord, channel the Word through me while I preach." You're looking at a "channel" when you look at me.

I recently visited one of those leading bookstores and discovered it had 167 different New Age titles in its New Age section. The Christian, religious section had 57 titles. Do you know why these occultic books are selling? Because people are hungry for the supernatural, and they haven't found it in the Church. You say, "Well, I know the denominations don't have God's power." Well, la-di-da. Neither do the Charismatics have it.

While Shirley MacLaine is the leading top-selling writer of New Age books, there are many, many more. Ruth Montgomery, a former journalist, has been declared "Herald of the New Age." Benjamin Creme, educator and claimed forerunner of the world's new, soon-coming occultic leader, has also written material that has influenced the thinking of many.

Marilyn Ferguson's book, *The Aquarian Conspiracy: Personal and Social Transformation in the 1980s,* is a detailed account of the current invasion of the New Age Movement into every arena of life — both public and private. And then there is J. Z. Knight, channel of the well-known entity, "Ramtha."

These and other New Age books are raking in the bucks as people willingly fork out their money to see a spiritual manifestation of some kind. One major New Age educator and psychologist says "channeling" is now reaching into every area of our culture. Their videos and cassette tape series of demons being "channeled" bring in an estimated $500 million a year — not to mention the sales of books, newsletters, and magazines in addition to this.

All of this reveals a real hunger on the part of a lost world looking for spiritual reality. Because they have not found supernatural reality in the Church, they have turned to another source, not realizing the great, great danger they are playing with. We, dear friends, are in tremendous need for a move of God that will confront a lost world and draw people to Jesus Christ.

The Great Deception

There is a great deception going on in the land today. This revival that we're boasting that's happening by the Holy Ghost is the most hollow revival that anyone has ever seen. It is overstretched; it is exaggerated. I believe not even 50 percent of the stories that I hear. It is an exaggeration.

I love ministry gifts, and I am one. But God is going to hold us accountable for exaggeration. How dare we report miracles when we do not know they can be substantiated? We need to stop this exaggeration, for as long as we pretend that we have power, we're never going to be in a position to really receive a genuine revival. And *real power* is on the way!

Show Biz Revival

The Church today has been duped. We think something really supernatural is going on. And I'm going to tell you something, Church: There's just a dribble here and a dribble there — and that is *all* there is. And a lot of the rest of it is show biz.

We need a Holy Ghost revival; we don't need some man-perpetrated move that has no substance to it. The reason people are running to the New Age is because the Church has not provided much genuine power. The world knows it's not there.

You say, "Now, Rick, aren't you kind of a defeatist?" No, I'm a *realist*. I'm telling you, there's not enough Holy Ghost power in my ministry. There's not. I wish there was more. There could be more.

You say, "Are you saying there are never any signs and wonders in your ministry?" No, there are signs and wonders.

Two big tumors just disappeared out of a little girl's tummy. Sure, I have signs and wonders. But, Church, do you know how big God is? *We haven't even touched the hem of His garments!* We haven't even started to touch the power that is available.

But we pretend. We say, "We're rich. We're full. We're blessed." Yet Jesus says, "You are wretched, you are miserable, you are poor, you are blind, you are naked" (Revelation 3:17). We need to come to grips with our powerlessness; then God can give us *His real power!* When it's a Holy Ghost revival, you're not going to have to wonder about it.

Do you know what gets me? It's when people come to healing meetings and claim to be healed. And you walk up to them and say, "Well, were you healed of cancer tonight?" "Uh huh." No excitement. No joy. In fact, their report is so sedate it makes you wonder if they're telling the truth. In the Bible, they shouted, they ran, they leaped, they praised God. I have a real hard time believing that person was touched by God.

I'm ready for something that will knock the socks off me, how about you? I keep having a dream — it's a repeating dream — and I know it's of the Holy Ghost. In this dream, I am in a meeting, and I'm preaching with a rich anointing when suddenly the power of God hits me, throws me across the room, slams me into the wall, and I'm thrown on the floor under the power of God.

And the whole congregation — smack! — is knocked right out of their chairs onto the floor. A visitation like this would be undeniable. That's what I want, don't you? The Church is starving for a *real* visitation of God's power.

Don't Fall on Me

For a long time, I told people they couldn't fall down in my prayer lines. Do you know why? It's now become a Pentecostal tradition. Can you imagine what God must think? We come and ask Him for help, and we think He can't do anything unless we fall on our backs. "God, I'll fall down if You'll help me."

A friend of mine said, "If we got rid of those ushers, we'd find out how many are really being slain by the power of God." Do you know why I'm mentioning that? Because we need to quit faking ourselves out. Now, that doesn't mean there isn't the genuine. There is the genuine. There is absolutely the genuine.

I was in a meeting in New York City where the Lord said, "Shut your eyes and just walk toward the people." I didn't know what He was going to do. I just shut my eyes. I started talking about the anointing, and I walked down the stage.

I was about to say, "Maybe the ushers should come forward." I said, "Now, just open your heart to the anointing," when I heard — wham, wham, wham, wham, wham, wham! I looked, and they were all down — no catchers. No catchers. Every one of them was touched by God that night. Every one of them. That's the kind of revival I want to be a part of.

Channeling the Power

We have a problem that's happening in the Church today. It's a real problem. I'm going to cover it in detail later on in this book. We have those people who are crazy hungry for power. And, thank God, we should be power hungry. The Holy Ghost is raw power. Our problem is, we don't know how to *channel* that power. I'm going to state it again: We don't know how to *channel* that power. We need to learn!

But let me tell you what people are saying. They're making a grave error which is going to lead the Church into a great, great, great catastrophe. People today are saying, "We've had enough of the Word. We don't need any more teaching. We've emphasized the Word. We labored in the

Word. It's time to get off the Word and go out into the realm of the Spirit."

Now listen, we need to go into the realm of the Spirit. I believe that. I've been there. I've had two visitations with the Lord. I've had a visitation with an angel. I've gone into the realm of the Spirit.

In 1985, I was transported by the Spirit from one place to another, and recently I had another extremely supernatural experience in God. But I want to tell you something: *If you abandon the Word and go out into the realm of the Spirit without the foundation of the Word, you're going to end up as messed up as the New Age.*

The Church is headed for catastrophe, and it's happening today. It is happening right now. *There will never be a day when we do not need the teaching of scripture — never! It is the foundation for the supernatural.*

But what about the New Age? Go back here to Second Timothy 3 and see what it says. It says that in the last days, there's going to be a revival of the occult, which means *there must then be a revival of the Holy Ghost to counteract this.* That's why I get excited. Look at verse 5. Verse 5 says, "Having a form of godliness, but denying the power thereof." It's describing the spirit of Jannes and Jambres, or occulticians.

Two major clues about this occult revival are the words "form" and "godliness." This word "form" is a Greek word, *morphosis.* It refers to an outward form or an outward sketch. It looks real. By looking at it, you can't tell that it's any different from the real thing.

But the whole idea of this word "form" is, all it has is an outward form. The substance is not the same. The substance is not right. In fact, the substance is all wrong. Outwardly, it looks right, it sounds right, it has the right form, it has the right markings. Everything looks right and, in fact, the Bible says "having a form of" — what? *"Godliness."*

Satan's New Disguise

What's happening today is, the devil has gotten smart, and he no longer is coming with a pitchfork and horns on his head. Today, he looks like godliness. He has disguised himself.

Do you know what the primary byword of the New Age Movement is? Are you ready for this? "Christ in you, the hope of glory." That's what New Age leaders say when they start their occultic seminars. They walk down off the stage, look at the people, and say, "You're so beautiful. I see Christ in you, the hope of glory."

That sounds like godliness, doesn't it? Except we're talking about a different Christ. They talk about a super, universal Christ-consciousness, Christ-spirit, or energy force which is in the universe and how we all need to plug into this Christ-consciousness. Sounds right, doesn't it?

In fact, if you were a young Christian, you might think you were dealing with Christians. But this Christ-consciousness has nothing to do with the Christ we know. This is the consciousness of Buddha, of Hinduism, of sorcery, of witches, and the cosmic consciousness that floats in the universe and we can tap into it, they say.

I was watching a television talk show program. The host had a whole panel of New Agers on his program. You should have heard what they were saying. It was this: "God is love. God is love. You don't need to be afraid of the walk-ins." That's what they call demons: walk-ins. Yes, that's exactly what they are. You open the door, and they'll walk in!

They were saying, "The walk-ins are part of the Christ-consciousness. They come to provide us with information and data that we need to direct our lives. And you've got to yield to the walk-ins, these entities. You've got to open yourself to them, and there's no fear, because God is love."

There was one Unity pastor on this program. Listen to what he said. He said, "Do you know what these fundamental Christians are? They are primitive. They are a group of people who must be done away with, because they believe there is only one way, and we know there is a collective consciousness, and we know we can all plug into it."

The Ultimate Deception

Ultimately, this New Age teaching teaches that we can all become God in our own right. And they're luring people with the power of signs and wonders.

In fact, do you know what they call Christians? They say Christians are *anti-Christ!* They're flipping that term around, and you ought to see the way they're using the Bible. They say, "If you want to know who the anti-Christ in the earth is, it's the Church, because the Church says there's just one way, when it's obvious that there are many ways."

They do not believe in a personal God but, rather, in a supreme energy force or super-consciousness that pervades the entire universe. This energy force they call a "Christ-consciousness." Their contention is that this super-consciousness is a force available to anyone who will attempt a contact — regardless of his belief system or religious commitment.

This, they say, is an energy force that reaches into Hinduism, Buddhism, Satanism, and even Christianity. All of these, according to New Age teaching, have the same potential to reach into the realm of the spirit to achieve "God-likeness."

According to this way of thinking, any group that actually believes there is just one way to God is primitive, backward, and behind the times. These primitive believers, New Age leaders say, are *anti-Christ.*

You say, "What?" That's right — they teach that *you* are anti-Christ — *you* are working against this super-consciousness that is trying to capture the world if you believe Jesus Christ is the only way to God. Christians, according to this New Age view, are the anti-Christs in the world. Talk about twisted thinking!

They say man is inherently good. According to them, everyone has the potential of God inside him — even stating that Hitler himself had one of the greatest potentials of godhood. They teach that with proper help, teaching, and assistance from spirit-guides, your inherent deity can come forth from within.

You say, "How in this world could they say Hitler had seeds of divinity within him?" They also say Lucifer has the seeds of divinity in him. In fact, when they come to the subject of Satan or Lucifer, they freely teach that Lucifer is another side of God.

Rather than fear him, they say, open your heart to him and receive him. He needs your love. They even quote scriptures at this point. "Perfect love casts out fear," they say. "By extending love to Lucifer, you will drive out unnecessary fear in your life. By accepting Lucifer, you will accept another part of God, and this will add to your own deity."

When we preach about sin, they again declare, "The day of Christianity is over. It is a religion of the past." You see, sin does not exist in a New Age way of thinking. To believe in sin is to label yourself as backward and against progress in the world.

To New Agers, anything is basically acceptable. There are no definite rights and wrongs — no set, fixed, firm standards. Whatever helps you achieve your fullest potential is right — regardless of past traditional thinking about sin — so do what you want to do. There is no such thing as sin. To believe in sin is a rejection of your own divinity, sovereignty, and control, they say.

These New Agers are "channeling" demon spirits at such a rate, it is alarming. What alarms me more than anything else is that they are doing a better job at channeling demons than we currently are at channeling the Holy Spirit!

Why? Because they are committed! They know there is a supernatural realm.

Being completely deceived by doctrines of demons, they are reaching into that realm to make a contact. Unfortunately, they have plugged into a real power source; however, this source will kill them and lead them into the pit of hell itself.

Kissing the Power Goodbye

Meanwhile, the Church world sits around and says, "Do you actually think you were transported by the Spirit? Come now, that is not intellectual." The Church has settled down into its brain. That's exactly what it's done. And it's kissed the power goodbye. The world is finding power without the Church, and I think that's sad. The New Agers are working signs and wonders. You say, "What! Without the Holy Spirit?"

There were signs and wonders *before* the Holy Spirit was poured out upon the Church. There were signs and wonders *before* Moses came on the scene. He knew signs and wonders before he knew God. Moses was an occultician. He was raised for only five years as a Hebrew. From the time he was five until he was forty, he was raised to be the next pharaoh of Egypt.

Moses was trained in the wisdom of the Egyptians. As head of state, Moses was to be the chief sorcerer of his land (just as the Queen of England is the head of the Anglican Church). In order to be the pharaoh, Moses had to know supernatural power.

When the Day of Pentecost came, why do you think it came with the power of signs and wonders? Because the occult already *had* signs and wonders. And, saints, here is the tragedy of our day: We currently do not have enough supernatural power flowing in the Church to confront an unbelieving world.

'Can You Show Me a Miracle?'

Moses said, "God, what do You mean, go to Pharaoh and say that You sent me? God, I know what he's going to say. Pharaoh is going to say, 'Well, we can work signs and wonders. Tell me, can you show me a miracle from your God?' " (Exodus 7:9.) Moses knew that unless he went in the power of signs and wonders, he had no credibility — nothing to substantiate his claims.

We're living in a day when we can no longer run up to someone with a tract, or put a book in someone's hand. This New Age Movement is growing so fast, they're going to look at us and say, "So what? Show me what your God can do."

The good news is, God's going to do it for us the same way He did it for Moses. And if the devil thinks he's got a revival meeting, *wait until you see the show that the Holy Ghost is about to put on!*

The Anointing of Satan

Now look at verse 5: "Having a form of godliness, but denying the power thereof: from such turn away." The idea is denying the power of God. This word "denying" is a Greek word, *arneomai,* which means, "I know the power exists, and I know it is real, but I am going to stop its operation." It refers to the deliberate refusal of God's power.

That is exactly what these occulticians — these New Agers of our day — are doing. They know God's power is real, and they are doing everything they can to stop it, because they are cooperating with the anointing of Satan.

The phrase "from such turn away" tells us we should not associate with these people, because deception is the name of their game. The phrase "from such turn away" is so strong in the Greek that it means, "Avoid them with horror. Run from them. Have nothing to do with them. Do nothing with them. Don't think about what they're saying. Don't be involved in what they're doing."

The idea is, "This is not a way for you to be thinking. This is not a thing for you to be pondering. Rather, you need to run, because deception is in their message."

Now look at verse 6: "For of this sort are they which creep into houses, and lead captive silly women laden with sins, led away with divers lusts." Notice the phrases "creep into" and "silly women." This sounds like a real attack on women, doesn't it?

The phrase "creep into" is actually the Greek word which means to put on a new set of clothes. If the devil came to you with a pitchfork in hand and horns on his head, would you let him into your house? Absolutely not. But what if he looked like God? What if he appeared as an angel of light?

Adam Wouldn't Buy It

The occult message in the last generation is going to be disguised in order that it can get into the house. And I want you to notice who the primary target is going to be: "silly women." This is not an attack against women. Satan has always known women were spiritually sensitive. He knew Adam would never buy his story, so he went for Eve. Eve was deceived. But the Bible says that Adam willingly sinned.

I just read some information from one of the "founding mothers" of the New Age Movement. She has an entire chapter in her book dedicated to the new woman. She says, "Women of our day will be the primary vehicle through which we will capture society with our new message."

And they're doing it through articles in magazines, advice columns, and periodicals. Everywhere you look, you seem to see a revival of horoscopes and palm readers. And do you know who buys most of that material? Unsanctified women who need direction in their life. You see, they're not willingly becoming involved with something bad. It's disguised. It looks like help, it looks like answers, so they're bringing it into their home.

Do you know what the intent of the devil is? To take them captive. The verse says this. Actually, the Greek says, "getting complete possession of." Satan wants to creep into our homes and eventually get complete possession of parents and children.

What Devil?

There is also a subtle deception to make us forget that there's something bad out there called the devil. The New Agers say, "Oh, but that's just a Christian concept. It's silly. These stupid, backward Christians are primitive. They think there's an ugly, old devil. Well, there's nothing like that. It's just a stupid, old concept." And they're wearing away at our beliefs, trying to make us forget the truth of scripture so we'll accept anything that can get into our house.

The next verse says, "Ever learning, and never able to come to the knowledge of the truth" (v. 7). That is the sad thing about the people in the New Age Movement. They are ever learning. They are disciples. They are constantly reading, trying to advance into new areas. They study, but they are in an unending cycle that leads them nowhere, because they will never come to the recognition of the real truth this way.

Verse 8 says, "Now as Jannes and Jambres withstood Moses, so do these also resist the truth...." You must especially see this word "so." This word is the Greek word *houtos*, which means "in the identical same way with the very same methods."

The last-days Church is going to experience in exact duplication what Moses experienced with the sorcerers. Now, that doesn't scare me. That excites me because, with the power of God, Moses vanquished them. And if the New Agers come with this same insidious message, that means *we are going to come with the same measure of God's power that Moses had.*

That's exactly what verse 8 says: "in the same ways, in the same methods, in the very same manner." Look at it: "Now as Jannes and Jambres withstood Moses, so will these men, in the same identical way, exactly the same way, a perfect duplication, resist the truth." The idea is, they're going to come against us with the power of signs and wonders. They're going to throw them in our face and say, "Can your Jesus do that?"

Notice what else verse 8 says: "men of corrupt minds." This word "corrupt" is the Greek word which means "completely ruined, depraved, and corrupted." "...men of corrupt minds, reprobate concerning the faith."

You may say, "Rick, this is a bleak picture you've painted of the world." That is an understatement. I want to tell you, the world is going to get dark, and the Church is going to get very bright. Are you excited to be a part of the Church? Something is about to happen! Gross darkness is going to come upon the earth, and the Lord is going to speak to the Church and say, "Arise, shine; for thy Light is come, and the glory of the Lord is risen upon thee" (Isaiah 60:1). And what a contrast there will be between darkness and light. I'm glad to be living in this day. Bring it on; it's fine with me. Glorious, radiant Light is going to shine on us very soon!

Verse 9 says, "But they shall proceed no further...." This word "proceed" means "to make an advance." The idea is this tremendous advance they have been making will suddenly stop. It will be cut off abruptly, and the Bible says, "their folly shall be manifest unto all men...." The word "folly" is the word *anoia*, which is the word "lack of intelligence."

Defective Signs and Wonders

In an instant, their corrupted, depraved mind and their blackened heart, which they disguised to look like God, are going to be exposed and cut off. And their lack of intelligence is going to be made manifest unto all men. This word "manifest" is the Greek word which means "it is manifested to be defective." Their way of thinking is defective. Their methods are defective. Their signs and wonders are defective.

Healing from the devil has a defect in it — you can be absolutely certain of this. A prophecy from the devil might have some truth in it, but it also has something in it that's going to catch and kill you. There is a defect in it.

The devil has nothing good in mind for you. His goal is deception. Whatever he wants to give you has a defect in it. You can be certain of it.

Now notice the remainder of verse 9: ". . . for their folly shall be manifest unto all men, as theirs also was." How was their folly manifested? How were Jannes and Jambres cut off? *We're talking about a confrontation of supernatural power: power for power.*

Go over to the Book of Exodus. I want you to see this as we're headed for the day of power. The Lord has more sense than we have. He knows what the world is going to ask, so look in Exodus 7, beginning with verse 8:

"And the Lord spake unto Moses and unto Aaron, saying, When Pharaoh [who is a type of the world] shall speak unto you, saying, Shew a miracle for you: then thou shalt say unto Aaron, Take thy rod, and cast it before Pharaoh, and it shall become a serpent.

"And Moses and Aaron went in unto Pharaoh, and they did so as the Lord had commanded: and Aaron cast down his rod before Pharaoh, and before his servants, and it became a serpent. Then Pharaoh also called the wise men and the sorcerers [bear in mind we're talking about Jannes and Jambres]: now the magicians of Egypt, they also did in like manner with their enchantments. For they cast down every man his rod, and they became serpents: but Aaron's rod swallowed up their rods" (vv. 8-12).

The Egyptian New Agers

God said, "I am going to show you I can outdo, outrun, overproduce anything the devil can do." Really, Egypt was the New Age of the old world. I tell you, God has a real sense of humor, because the serpent was the symbol of all the Egyptian gods. By doing this, do you know what God said? "My power is going to slap your occultic power right in the face. I'm going to gobble it up." And God devoured their god.

Do you know that every one of these things God touched was something they worshipped and was an integral part of their occultic religion? They believed the Nile was the mother of the gods. Everything that was supernatural came out of the Nile, they believed, so God defiled it with blood. They would go to the Nile, which was their mother of the gods, and it was defiled, and they couldn't get rid of the blood.

God ate up the serpent, God touched their "mama," the Nile, and now God's going to ruin something else. Go over to verse 22: "And the magicians of Egypt did so with their enchantments." They reproduced what God did. This was *power for power!*

Look what God does in the next chapter of Exodus. Watch as God touches the idolatry of man. I love this eighth chapter, because the Egyptians worshipped frogs, and God says, "I'm going to go get their frog god next!"

Start with verse 1: "And the Lord spake unto Moses, Go unto Pharaoh, and say unto him, Thus saith the Lord, Let my people go, that they may serve me. And if thou refuse to let them go, behold, I will smite all thy borders with frogs: And the river shall bring forth frogs" — how much? — "abundantly, which shall go up and come into thine house, and into thy bedchamber, and upon thy bed, and into the house of thy servants, and upon thy people, and into" — what? — "thy ovens [How would you like baked frog?], And into thy kneadingtroughs:

42

"And the frogs shall come up both on thee, and upon thy people, and upon all thy servants. And the Lord spake unto Moses, Say unto Aaron, Stretch forth thine hand with thy rod over the streams, over the rivers, and over the ponds, and cause frogs to come up upon the land of Egypt" (vv. 1-5).

'Stretch Forth Thy Rod'

Saints, we are headed for a day when God is going to speak to the Church. We are going to hear Him say, "Stretch forth thy rod." Moses' rod was just an ordinary old rod. He'd had it for many years, and he'd used it every day. Yet, *Moses never knew what power could come out of that rod.*

In the same way, God's rod — the Holy Spirit — has been a part of our experience for many years. We've enjoyed the Spirit and allowed Him to work in our lives. Yet, we have never comprehended the full authority and power available in Him.

Just as Moses threw his rod before Pharaoh, we are going to hear God tell us, "Throw the Spirit's power before the world!" *A new day of supernatural power is about to be unleashed in the Church. God is going to prove who He is!*

Now notice what God did in verse 6: "And Aaron stretched out his hand over the waters of Egypt; and the frogs came up, and covered the land of Egypt."

Notice how stupid the occulticians are: "And the magicians did so with their enchantments, and brought up frogs upon the land of Egypt" (v. 7). They could duplicate the miracle, but guess what? They couldn't get rid of the frogs! Only God could get rid of the frogs. Their frog god was destroyed. They prayed, "Oh, dear frog, please go home," but the frog god had no power.

The frog problems became so bad that frogs were found in their ovens! "Ovens" were clay vessels. You padded dough along the inside of the vessel, put it into the sand, and when the sun beat upon the sand, the hot sand would bake that dough. When the top of the vessel was opened, you would find baked bread. Only like sausage bread, this was *frog bread*. Frogs were into everything!

Do you know what God did next? He struck the lice. (We're talking about creeping things.) And the Bible says that everything in the land of Egypt that was dust turned into lice. Now what country are we talking about? Egypt. How much dust is there in Egypt? A lot. All the dust became lice.

That means the dirt in the flower pot suddenly turned into lice. That means if the floor of your house was a dirt floor, your whole floor was covered with lice. Rather than walking across a dirt street, now the dirt was creeping underneath your feet. Lice were everywhere. If you had dirt on you, you had lice on you.

The Bible says we were made out of the dust of the earth. And it says here in Exodus that there was not only lice on the Egyptians; lice were *on* them and *in* them. In fact, lice were on and in both man and beast. Wasn't that a happy little situation?

Verses 18 and 19 show us the day that we're headed for: "And the magicians did so with their enchantments to bring forth lice, but they could not: so there were lice upon man, and upon beast. Then the magicians said unto Pharaoh, This is the finger of God...."

And power for power, God proved He could outdo, overproduce, outrun, do anything bigger and better than Satan ever dreamed.

Two Kinds of Channels

God needs only one thing — just one thing. All He needs is a *channel*. What's a channel? It's a tube through which water flows, or it's a conduit through which electricity flows. Do you know that, through your spirit, that's exactly what you are?

God channels His power through your spirit, past your soul, and out your body. All He needs is someone who is a channel.

He needs someone who is yielded; someone who will say, "Make me a channel of blessing today. Make me a channel, a blessing, I pray."

Just as Moses became a channel for God's power, God wants to pour His power through the Church today. Yes, God wants to outdo, outproduce, outrun, and prove that His power is the greatest in the universe!

A Holy Ghost revival like the world has never seen *must* occur before the coming of the Lord. *The Church is about to become a gigantic Holy Ghost channel!*

Here is an example of a person who *is* a channel for a demon entity. While this particular New Age leader grew up in a deeply religious church background, she had never seen a real manifestation of God's power.

Standing in her home one night, a demon spirit — she says it was a brilliant, beautiful, heavenly light — manifested in front of her. This spirit, whom she calls an entity, identified itself as a spirit-being that had been on the earth for thousands of years. This entity (demon) spoke to her and said, "If you will yield to me, I will work through you and make you a channel of blessing to the world." She yielded.

Today she packs auditoriums. Thousands come to hear her and attend her meetings. She charges enormous prices per seat. Under the influence of this demon spirit, another entity begins to speak through her. She gives counsel, she gives lectures, and she tells the future with, I might add, some accuracy. It is *demonic* entertainment and *demonic* direction.

We, not demon-possessed people, are supposed to be the oracles in the earth. God wants the Church to be a channel. He wants *you* to be a channel!

The great thing is, if you're built on a firm foundation of the Word, you're not going to fly off into something that's weird and wrong. You've already got a foundation. You've got maturity. You know what's good. You know what's right. You're not going to mess up. If anyone is in a position to be used in the supernatural, it's a person with a foundation in the Word. It's those people with no foundation who are going to mess up.

Only those with the foundation of the Word are really in a position to channel the power of God.

Saints, I cannot lay my hands on you and give you a Holy Ghost revival. Do you know how much God wants to give a revival? Do you know how much God wants to visit us with an unmistakable, undeniable visitation? God is crying out for a body of people who will be a channel for His power. All He needs is a yielded vessel.

O Jesus, make me a channel of blessing today. Make me a channel of blessing, I pray!

Rick Renner's Expanded Translation of Second Timothy 3:1-5
(Freely Translated)

Come to grips with certain facts; in the very last times treacherous, dangerous, high-risk periods that produce great hurt and harm will come.

For men will become selfish and self-centered — inordinately in love with themselves, inordinately materialistic and in love with money, willing to exaggerate the facts — even willing to lie and stretch the truth if it will bring them the gain they are wanting; they will be marked by a feeling of superiority; abusive, harsh, blasphemous language will be theirs; children will be unpersuadable, disobedient — beyond control; generally speaking, people will be ungrateful — they will be morally lewd, loose, and nasty.

A normal love for family will disappear; people will become irreconcilable — unable to come to terms with one another; they will almost seem as the devil himself — accusing and slandering; they will be uncontrollable in nearly every way — with sex, greed, money, credit, government — appetites of every sort will go to the farthest extreme, producing a people who are fierce — untamable — beyond control — almost uncivilized; this will be a day when there will be no laws for the good people.

Oath breakers, a generation of reckless, hasty, rash decisions — yes, temporarily making things better, but in the long run harmful and incredibly hurtful decisions; they will swell and roll in as overwhelmingly as a hurricane, attempting to radically change and alter everything along their way — but just as quickly as a hurricane hits, just that quickly they will blow away. These will be temporal-minded people — completely deceived — in love with moments and lifestyles of pleasure — their love for pleasure will far outmeasure any love for God. In comparison, love for God will amount to nothing — this they exchanged for their own comfort.

They will come to possess an outward appearance of godliness — making themselves to look and sound like God, though their inward substance is defective; they will do all in their power to deny and stop the operation of God's power. FROM SUCH, turn away with legitimate horror!

Chapter 4
The Occultic Surge

This third chapter of Second Timothy deals primarily with last-day occurrences. Yes, these problems were present in Timothy's day, but notice that Second Timothy 3:1 specifically mentions "the last days."

It reads, ". . . in the last days perilous times shall come." And that word "perilous" is the Greek word *chalepos*, which refers to something that is "treacherous, dangerous, and harmful," eventually bringing great hurt to those who live in the last days.

Actually, the Greek says, "perilous *times.*" The word "times" refers to set periods of times, like decades. The whole idea is that one decade will produce its own measure of damage. Then the next decade will produce its own new philosophy which will hurt the standards of the world — and the next decade, and the next, and the next.

We saw this happen in the twenties, thirties, forties, fifties, sixties, and seventies. Now we're in the eighties, headed for the nineties, and the nineties will be a day when universities across the United States and the world will begin to declare the decline of Christianity. We're living in a world that is becoming a lawless place. We must have a supernatural visitation of God's power to confront the world!

The Spirit of Jannes and Jambres

One of the primary results of all these decades working together to produce harm is the New Age Movement, which I call *the spirit of Jannes and Jambres.*

49

We're talking about witchcraft and sorcery. These things are abundant in our land today. If you live in a city that is highly religious and full of all kinds of churches, you may not be as aware of it as much as if you were traveling all the time.

When I go from city to city to city, I make it a point to find bookstores. You can always tell by bookstores what's going on in the community, because you can learn what people are reading and how people are thinking. I also go right to the Yellow Pages to find out how many Unity churches (not Unitarian; *Unity*) and how many New Age churches there are. When you travel this country as I do, you'll find that this New Age Movement is moving at an alarming rate.

In fact, in Second Timothy 3:13 it says, "Evil men and seducers shall wax worse and worse, deceiving, and being deceived." And that word "seducers" is the Greek word *goes,* which refers to someone who uses incantations, sorcery, magic, and spells.

The Bible says that evil men and seducers — those who use sorcery — "shall wax worse and worse." This is in the comparative in the Greek. The idea is, "Timothy, if you think it's bad now, wait till the last days. It will be far, far worse then than it is now. Seducers will abound."

Paul says this occultic surge will build *slowly* in the last days. In fact, it will build so slowly that people won't even recognize it. Until recent years, most Christians didn't even take the devil seriously. They laughed at "extremists" who believe in an aggressive devil and demonic activity. "Witches? Oh, pooh-pooh that. There's nothing to witches," they used to say.

The Satanic Undercurrent

But there has been an undercurrent of satanic activity during recent years. Just like the Bible says, all of a sudden, almost out of the clear blue (no one will understand how it happened so fast) — zoom! — this thing will cut through, clear to the worst stage. The occult has made an advance upon civilization that is mind-boggling.

The idea of Second Timothy 3:13 is that a worldwide impact of sorcery will come upon the earth, upon education, upon government, upon homes, upon families, upon children. This is even invading our home every Saturday morning. If you don't believe me, turn on your television set and watch the cartoons. They are full of New Age occultism.

Most new cartoons are undoubtedly New Age occultism. If you are a parent with young children, it would be good for you to set aside several Saturday mornings to watch cartoons and see this for yourself. Seducing spirits are trying to grab hold of our children.

You say, "Rick Renner, you're just an alarmist!" Someone *needs* to sound the alarm. The Church *needs* to wake up to what is happening. This occultic surge is happening right under our own noses!

What is really tragic, the New Age Movement is producing genuine signs and wonders. They know how to produce the supernatural! They are proficient at healing. Do you know why? They have *committed their life* to the act of sorcery.

A New Name for Mediums

Mediums today have thrown out that old name "medium." Today they've picked up a new name. Mediums are now called "channels." As I noted in Chapter 3, this is particularly bothersome to me, because I grew up in a church where we sang, "Make me a *channel* of blessing today. Make me a *channel* of blessing, I pray." And do you know what the very next statement in this song is? "My life *possessing*."

That's exactly what the Holy Spirit wants to do! He wants to *possess* us! He wants to *channel* Himself through us!

But the New Age, the occult, has picked up that word "channel." They are becoming excellent channels of demon spirits. Increasingly, channeling is becoming popular and acceptable. It has been stated that channels (mediums) are quickly becoming replacements for psychiatrists. One report has estimated that Los Angeles alone now has more than 1,000 active channelers.

Channelers are the latest craze in Hollywood. Imagine people running to mediums, receiving counseling from mediums, and referring their associates to mediums. This, of course, would not happen if they understood the real dangers of occultism. Channelers are "in."

Channelers are now a frequent and popular subject on television talk shows. I have personally watched their appearances on Oprah Winfrey and Phil Donahue. Smaller, less-known talk shows have also made these channelers a regular part of their program. It seems the public is developing a strange preoccupation with these occultic practices which the Bible plainly forbids.

Deuteronomy 18:9-12 says: "When thou art come into the land which the Lord thy God giveth thee, thou shalt not learn to do after the abominations of those nations. There shall not be found among you any one that maketh his son or his daughter to pass through the fire, or that useth divination, or an observer of times, or an enchanter, or a witch, Or a charmer, or a consulter with familiar spirits, or a wizard, or a necromancer. For all that do these things are an abomination unto the Lord: and because of these abominations the Lord thy God doth drive them out from before thee."

A New Name for Demons

My wife and I were watching one of these major television talk shows. The subject of the program was the New Age Movement and channeling. There was a whole panel of New Age channelers — mediums — men and women who had completely committed their lives for the purpose of channeling entities. Again, that's the new word for demons.

They are also now called spirit-guides, spirit-writers, spirit-assistants, spirit-helpers, and spirit-friends. One leading New Age leader calls these spirits walk-ins. (As I stated earlier, if you willingly open the door to these demons, you can be sure — they will walk right in!)

Suddenly the talk show host turned to one of these men who was supposed to be a superb channeler and said, "Well, tell me, could you open yourself up to this entity (demon) right now, and could this entity begin talking to us on TV?" The channeler said, "Go to a commercial break, and while you're in the break, I will start meditating."

When the cameras were turned back on him, this man was sitting slumped in his chair. A camera zoomed in on him, and suddenly his body began shaking violently. It looked like a supernatural force was literally pushing itself through his body and out of him.

When he lifted his head, his face didn't look the same. His countenance was different. He began speaking in a broken European accent — and this man grew up in California! This was not an act: This man was channeling a demon spirit right on television!

The audience began to exude excitement and ask questions. Under the influence of a demon spirit, this man began giving demonic advice. I watched as he yielded himself to a foreign entity (demon), and that entity began to speak through him and answer their questions. While I was shocked to see this on national television, it was not the last time I saw this on national television. "Channeling" is now a common occurrence on television talk shows.

I was in a bookstore on the East Coast, and I went into the religious section. There I saw a book entitled *Prophetic Sayings From Immanuel*. That sounds like a good book, doesn't it? So I picked up this book and opened it, expecting to read some words from the Lord. However, these were the strangest prophetic sayings I've ever heard our Immanuel say!

I turned to the front of the book to read the preface, and discovered — *this* Immanuel was not *our* Immanuel. This was an entity named Immanuel which possessed a housewife. Through her, he began penning these things.

Here is another interesting point. While some of these entities indeed have come with strange, far-out names, such as Ekton, Mafu, Seth, and Ramtha, there are also entities with Bible names. This plainly is an attempt to attract those with a religious background who would never feel good about listening to "Ekton," "Mafu," or "Ramtha."

Imagine demon entities identifying themselves as: Jonah, Isaiah, Elijah, Lazarus, Immanuel, Jesus, or Paul. If you were a new client for a medium, having a spirit named "Lazarus" or "Jesus" or "Paul" might ease your fear a little. Who knows, it might be the Lazarus, Jesus, or Paul of the Bible! This, again, is an attempt to lure people into this deadly demonic web of deception.

Demonic Invasion Ahead for the Church

While a demonic invasion is occurring in the world today, with worldwide implications, First Timothy 4:1 declares a *similar* demonic invasion will occur *within* the Church in the last days. This verse says, "Now the Spirit speaketh expressly, that in the latter times some shall depart from the faith, giving heed to seducing spirits, and doctrines of devils."

Here, Paul is not talking about the world. He is talking about activity on *the inside of the Church*. Notice that phrase "latter times." This unquestionably refers to the *last* of the last days. The word "last" is the Greek word *husterois*. *Husterois* always refers to the *end* of a thing. In this sense, the *end*, or the *last* of the last days.

Isn't this interesting? In Second Timothy 3:1, the Holy Spirit tells us what phenomena will occur in the world during the last, difficult days. Now, in First Timothy 4:1, He tells us what *will* occur *inside* the Church during these same last days.

While a real, genuine move of the Holy Spirit will occur in the last days, the Bible says a mass invasion of seducing spirits will also attempt to move inside the Church!

"Now the Spirit speaketh *expressly....*" This word "expressly" is the Greek word *rhetos*. *Rhetos* refers to something spoken clearly and unmistakably. You could translate it, "The Spirit speaks with *vivid illustration.*" Or, "The Spirit speaks in undeniable terms." Or, "The Spirit speaks unmistakably."

Seducing Spirits and Doctrines of Demons

This word from the Spirit is absolutely emphatic! It *is* going to happen. It *cannot* be escaped. Some *will* be seduced by spirits and doctrines of demons. Some *will* depart from the faith. The Spirit makes this emphatically clear. He has spoken this in undeniable terms.

Why will some depart from the faith? Look at what it says: "Now the Spirit speaks in *clear words,*" or "The Spirit *speaketh expressly* in *undeniable terms* that in the last of the last times some shall depart from *the faith.*"

This phrase "the faith" is used in the objective sense. In other words, it doesn't refer to raw faith — like faith to work miracles, or faith to heal the sick. This refers to *the* Christian faith. This refers to the Bible and the basic tenets of scripture. This refers to the sound teaching of the Word of God.

The Holy Ghost predicts that in the last days, there will be some within the Church who will step away from sound teaching of *doctrine*. What we mean here is the body of Christian truth: the Bible and the Christian faith.

These people will begin to turn away from these basic elements that make Christianity what it is. They will no longer view "the faith" as something important. Rather than being important, they will view it as something rather boring, dull, and dead.

Notice, I didn't say they were going to depart *from Jesus*. I said they would depart *from doctrine*, or *the faith*. We're talking about people who lose a taste for the Word. They lose a taste for the body of Christian doctrine, and they turn away from it.

A Departure From Jesus

In reality, this is a departure from Jesus. This will not be their intention; however, a departure from the Word is always a departure from Jesus.

Especially notice the word "depart." We need to take note of it. This word "depart" is the Greek word which means "to step away from." This doesn't necessarily indicate a mental decision to step away from "the faith." Rather, this describes a person who moves from one position to another *so slowly* that he isn't even aware that he is making a *transition*. Yet a transition is occurring — very, very *slowly*. His position is changing. His thinking is *slowly* changing. One small step after another, he is *slowly withdrawing*. He is *departing* from the faith.

Why would people do that? This tells of a day when people are tired of the Word. To them, the Word is boring. They've heard so much Word, they're nearly choking on it. Now they are ready for some *action*. They are tired of hearing. Now they want *experience*.

The Scriptural Foundation

It is good to desire *experience*. We desperately need a demonstration of God's power today — and it will happen.

However, God will *never* lead us away from His Word — NEVER! Thank God for experience! Thank God for the realm of the Spirit! But these things will *never* take the place of scripture — NEVER! The scripture *must* be the foundation for these experiences.

We must be very careful today. *An inordinate desire for the supernatural may be a result of seducing spirits who are trying to draw us away from scripture with the sensational and the spectacular.*

What does the next part of the verse say? "...giving heed to seducing spirits, and doctrines of devils." Look again at that phrase "giving heed." This is very important. This phrase "giving heed" is the Greek word which conveys the idea of turning your thoughts in another direction. It's the Greek word which means to consider other options.

This describes a people who are opening *their minds* to new thoughts and new possibilities. They've had the Word, and they think they know everything there is in the Word. They're not satisfied with the Word, so they say, "Surely there's got to be more than this."

Beyond the Bible?

For example, a major ministry recently said, "In the next move of God we won't need the Bible. We will move beyond the Bible. We've had all the Word we need. Now we're moving beyond — into the realm of the Spirit." I want to tell you, this borders on "doctrines of devils." This ministry must be aware, lest it *depart* from "the faith"!

I just read a book which said that the day of teaching is over! "We've had all the Word that we need," the book read. "We're so taught we don't even know what to do with it, so it's time to *leave teaching* and *move out* into the dimension of the Spirit."

I saw a newsletter of another major ministry, saying the Church is so taught, it doesn't need to be taught anymore. I wonder what churches they're going to! Few churches in the country are taught that well. There is a *tremendous* need for good teachers today. In fact, so much bad teaching is currently being circulated that good teaching is becoming rare and more important all the time.

If you're a good teacher, your ministry is going to be blessed. Because there's such a lack of people who really come with the substance of the Word, when people hear it, they're thrilled.

Some people are deluded into thinking we have a great deal of Word teaching in the land today. Yes, there has been *some* good Word in the land. God has given some excellent teachers to the Church. But generally speaking, you do not discover this across the broad spectrum.

The Mark 11:23,24 Movement

While the Word Movement was good, it was not really a *Word* movement. It's been a Mark 11:23,24 movement. Thank God for Mark 11:23,24. Thank God for the revelation He gave Kenneth E. Hagin. It changed my life. It was an ingredient that we sorely needed. But all it is, is *an ingredient.*

What you find is, many churches have majored on that one ingredient as though that is all there is. Many know nothing but Mark 11:23,24. Others have majored on prayer. Thank God for prayer. It, too, is *one* ingredient. Some have majored just on intercession. It, too, is *one* ingredient. We must, however, be founded on the Word! *The Word must be our foundation.*

Many don't know what the *doctrine of sanctification* or *redemption* or *justification* is. Yet, this major ministry put out a newsletter that said, "The day of teachers is over." Do you know, as long as there are new babies being born, there's going to be a day for teachers?

Some say, "But, Rick, the Bible says we need to go on unto perfection." They even quote Hebrews 6:1,2:

"Therefore leaving the principles of the doctrine of Christ, let us go on unto perfection; not laying again the foundation of repentance from dead works, and of faith toward God, Of the doctrine of baptisms, and of laying on of hands, and of resurrection of the dead, and of eternal judgment."

Could You Pass the Doctrine Test?

Their contention is, we've labored on the elementary principles too long; it's now time to move on! Is that right? Let's see how well we've covered the elementary principles. If given a test on these doctrines, could you pass it with flying colors? Could you pass it at all?

How would you fare if given a test on Biblical Repentance? The Doctrine of Baptisms? The Doctrine of Eternal Judgment? Or, how about the Doctrine of the Laying on of Hands? Or, the Doctrine of Resurrection?

I agree, it is time for us to move on. However, the Bible says, "For when the time ye ought to be teachers, ye have *need* that one teach you again which be the first principles of the oracles of God; and are become such as have need of milk, and not of strong meat" (Hebrews 5:12). The day of teaching is far from being over!

Paul's Last Request: The Word

The Apostle Paul was in a prison cell. A short time later, they were going to take his head off his shoulders out on the Ostian Way, west of Rome. He was never going to preach another sermon. He was never going to see another face. Do you know what his last request was? "...when thou comest, bring with thee...the books, but especially the parchments" (2 Timothy 4:13). Do you know what he's referring to? Old Testament scriptures.

I don't know about you, but I think if they were going to take my head off, and I was never going to preach another sermon or minister to another crowd in my life, I might be tempted to think, "Why study? In a short time, I'm going to know everything anyway!" Yet *the day of the Word* was not over for the Apostle Paul's life. He still had two more months and, therefore, he still needed the Word for two more months. I hope you see the importance of scripture. Even Paul needed to be taught.

This is how I would translate First Timothy 4:1:

"Now the Spirit speaketh expressly, in undeniable terms, in words that are absolutely clear, that in the last of the last times some will slowly distance themselves from the basic teaching of scripture, thinking that it is boring, giving heed, turning their ears to another thought, turning their mind to another way of thinking, considering another option, looking for something better. They will turn from the faith, *giving heed to seducing spirits and doctrines of devils.*"

How To Guard Against Seducing Spirit

The word "seducing" is extremely important. This is the Greek word *planos*. This is what I would call a word of seduction. It is not outright *deception;* it is *seduction.* It is something that looks and sounds right. Everything about it looks right. You just know that finally you found a new revelation that's right!

Or, here is someone you can trust! Here is someone who really knows something about the supernatural! Now we need to listen to what he's saying!

Actually, this word "seducing" means "to take you by the hand and to lead you so slowly off track that you don't even realize you're going off track." You trust the person who is leading you. He's been around a long time. But he slowly begins to lead you off track. The person whom the seducing spirit is working through is deceived, too. He believes he is headed in the right direction.

Signs & Wonders – The Word = 0

Do you know what always accompanies seducing spirits? Signs and wonders. Any time there are signs and wonders, you can attract a crowd — any time. Jesus multiplied the fish, had a big fish fry, and attracted thousands and thousands. It's when He brought them the Word that they turned away from Him! Signs and wonders without the Word equal nothing in God's sight. The occult can do that!

We're talking about seducing spirits and doctrines of devils or demons. Now look at the word "doctrines," because this is the Greek word *didaskalia*. The word *didasko* means "I teach," and the word *kalia* is from *kalos*, which means "good or beautiful." When you put these two words together, the word *didaskalia* refers to a teacher who is *proficient*.

He (or she) is not just a teacher; he is a *good* teacher. This is someone who really knows how to teach. He really knows how to preach. This is someone who knows how to handle himself in the pulpit. He is an excellent speaker and an excellent teacher. The problem is, he's using those gifts to lead people *away from the Word* and lead them into *the spectacular and sensational.*

Please understand — I'm not against the spectacular. I want you to know that Rick Renner is *not against* the spectacular. Rick Renner is *not against* the Holy Spirit. I'm *not against* miracles. I'm *not against* signs and wonders. No, I'm *for* all those things, and we need all those things. But we need *the real thing*; we don't need an *imitation* or a *fabrication*.

How do you know that you have the *real* move of God, not an imitation or a fabrication? *The Word.* The Word and the Spirit agree.

The Formula for Error

The Spirit says in undeniable terms — in absolutely clear words — that in the last times, some will shuck the Word and just take the things of the Spirit, and that is going to produce error. That always produces error.

Where people let loose of the Word and float out into the realm of the Spirit, they never come back. We must maintain a balance between the Word and the Spirit.

You see, I'm not saying that we shouldn't have signs and wonders. *We should.* We need a Holy Ghost revival with more power than any power we've ever seen. We've got to confront the powers of the New Age. We've got to confront the powers of the occult.

If they can raise the dead, then we need to know how to raise the dead, too. And, by the way, they *are* practicing the resurrection of the dead right now in a major New Age group. They're very serious about this thing.

Now let's look at the solution Paul gives to Timothy about this problem in First Timothy 4:6. Verse 6 says, "If thou put the brethren in remembrance of these things, thou shalt be a good minister of Jesus Christ, nourished up in the words of faith and of good doctrine, whereunto thou hast attained."

What we want to know is: Is this man leading me into the deep things of God that are right, or is this man leading me into a doctrine that will produce error? Where is this man leading me?

How To Recognize a Good Ministry

Verse 6 tells us how to recognize a good ministry. Look at the phrase "If thou put the brethren in remembrance of these things...." This phrase is actually from the Greek word *hupotithemi. Hupo* means "underneath," and *tithemi* means "to place, position, or lay a foundation." When you put these two words together, it means literally, "If you build a firm foundation under the brethren, thou shalt be a good minister of Jesus Christ." This is a reference to laying a foundation of the Word underneath the brethren.

It is fine to have the supernatural, but you must have a foundation for that supernatural to stand on! If there is no foundation under the brethren, then they will be prone to go into error. So Paul says, "Here's how you know if you're dealing with a good ministry, a bad ministry, or if *you* are a good ministry or a bad ministry: What are you doing with the foundation?" Foundation.

If I floated into a meeting on a cloud and floated around the room for four different nights, it might be exciting, but it wouldn't necessarily be good. There must be foundation along with the spectacular. That is what the Word is saying.

Incredible Experiences

I've had some incredible experiences, so one night I decided I'd be spectacular and tell everyone how they could plug into the realm of the Spirit. (Now I'm careful about doing this, because when I shared these experiences, I was humiliated by what the pastor said at the end of the meeting.)

I shared about how I'd been transported by the Spirit one night from one state to another state. Then I shared how I went to another country in the Spirit one night earlier this year.

In the middle of the night, I found myself standing at the front door of a house, and I knocked. An older man, probably in his fifties, opened the door, looked at me, and said, "We've been waiting for you all day." He said, "Come in. We have your coat ready. We've been waiting on you to get here. Now we're going to go."

He continued, "I can't go the same way I went the last time, because the last time, they almost caught me." And he gave me a coat that looked like it was made out of canvas or something heavy. Maybe it was wool, but it was shabby, it was gray, and it was depressing looking. His home was depressing looking, too. There wasn't much there.

The clouds outside were gray. The scenery looked oppressive. The ground was almost frozen. There was snow, there was ice, and the trees were sparse.

The man said, "We're going to go this way, because I can't go the way that I went the last time. We're going to walk through the trees over here, and we're going to walk across a frozen pond." We began walking. We walked through the trees. We walked across three frozen ponds.

The man said, "Now, just over the hill is the town where we're going." And he showed me that town. He said, "That's it — that house right over there — we're going to go up those steps. We're going to have the meeting in the basement of that house."

As we went up the steps, I remember seeing moss-like lichen or something similar growing on the side of the steps. We went into the basement of that home, and there was a room that was not very big at all — maybe 25 feet long and 15 feet wide. And crammed into this room were about fifty people. They were wearing black, gray, and other dark-colored clothing, the women with little scarves over their heads and the husbands with little hats on their heads. They were huddled together, waiting for someone to read the Bible to them.

It was Siberia. How did I know it was Siberia? First, because of my conversation with the man I had been with. Second, a week later, I walked into a hotel room where a public education program was on television. I sat down to watch, and I saw those sparse trees. It looked exactly like the place where I had been.

I said, "Denise, that's Siberia." My little boy looked up at me and said, "Daddy, you haven't even been there. How do you know what it is?" It was Siberia.

Do you know what the pastor said the night when I shared that testimony? He said, "Well, it's been interesting tonight. We've heard how Rick Renner has traveled all over the world without an airplane, flying through the air." Those were his words.

Stories Require Substance

Do you know what I realized? You've got to give people *substance*. You can't just give them stories. *You've got to build a foundation.* And if they don't have a foundation, then they don't need to be hearing some of these experiences, because *experience without foundation will lead you into error.* On the other hand, *the Word without experience will leave you doubting.* So we must have both!

And Paul said to Timothy, "It's fine to have the experience, but make sure you build a foundation." You must never leave the teaching of the Word. You must never leave a strong body of Christian faith and Christian doctrine. We *must* have these things.

If you're in a church where foundational doctrines are being laid week after week, you are blessed! I'm going to tell you, some of those people who have left the Word behind are really spiritual "spooks." *Attempting to function in deep Holy Spirit manifestations without foundation will leave you floating into error.*

Do you know what some of these people say about churches with strong Bible teaching ministries? "No supernatural over there; just Word. That's all. Don't go. All you get is the Word."

Foundation for Revival

A church that has a foundation in the Word is one type of church that is ready to receive a supernatural move of the Holy Ghost, because it has a foundation. If you want a real, powerful, supernatural move of the Holy Ghost, build a foundation in the Word!

Chapter 5
God Is Watching

We're looking at an end-time phenomenon *within* the Church. In light of all this activity, Paul says in Second Timothy 4:1-5, "I charge thee therefore before God, and the Lord Jesus Christ, who shall judge the quick and the dead at his appearing and his kingdom; Preach the word; be instant in season, out of season; reprove, rebuke, exhort with all longsuffering and" — what? — "doctrine.

"For the time will come when they will not endure sound" — what? — "doctrine; but after their own lusts shall they heap to themselves teachers, having itching ears; And they shall turn away their ears from the truth, and shall be turned unto fables. But watch thou in all things, endure afflictions, do the work of an evangelist, make full proof of thy ministry."

Notice verse 1 says, "I charge thee therefore before God, and the Lord Jesus Christ...." You've got to remember Paul is talking to a preacher.

Do you feel called to ministry? Then this verse is for you. If you want to make sure that you are not a teacher who is going to lead people into error, then you need to pay heed to these verses and obey them. If you do, you can be sure you are a good minister of Jesus Christ.

The word "charge" is the Greek word *diamarturomai*. This word was originally used to swear in public officials or those who presided over the affairs of men. It's very important that this word be used for a preacher, because a preacher indeed is a public official. He is one who presides and has influence over the affairs of men.

Invitation to the Divine

The word "charge" *(diamarturomai)* always invoked the special attention of the gods. In fact, if you were taking the oath of public office, this word actually invited the Greek gods to come and witness the public ceremony.

This meant the oath was extremely serious. The gods were watching. They were listening. They were waiting to see if you would carry out your new commitment. Did you take the oath seriously? Therefore, it was the most solemn charge that could be given.

You, as a minister, are taking an oath that you promise you will never, never, never, never break. You are laying your life on the line. You are saying, "Yes, yes, yes, I take that oath! Yes, I will do that! I will do that! Yes! I will never break it as long as I live!" *We are talking about a commitment.*

Paul says, "I charge thee therefore *before.*" Understand the word "before," because it again supports the seriousness of a preacher's commitment. This word "before" is the Greek word *enopion,* which means "within the eyesight of someone else." A literal translation could be, "within the full view of God's eyes...." The idea is, this oath is made in front of God so that He can watch you do it from beginning to end.

Timothy is taking an oath. We find out that someone is attending this swearing in that Timothy is taking. I want you to notice that it's *not* the Church that is listening. Who is Timothy taking this oath within the eyesight of? God and the Lord Jesus Christ.

The whole idea is, "Son, you'd better mean business, because God Himself is looking in on this meeting of your ordination. He is watching you take this oath." That would make a real difference in your commitment, wouldn't it?

What if you looked up, the ceiling was gone, and two giant eyes were looking down on you? That's exactly the idea. "Buddy, you'd better understand — this is so serious that God Himself is listening. God is watching. And God is waiting to see if you're going to be faithful." This is the oath that every Gospel minister takes when he says yes to the call of God.

A Surprise Appearance

Now look at verse 1 once again: "I charge thee therefore before God, and the Lord Jesus Christ, who shall judge the quick and the dead at his appearing and his kingdom." Notice the word "appearing." It's the Greek word *epiphaneia*. This word was always used by Greeks to describe a surprise appearance by a Greek god.

Two things are confirmed in this verse. First, the deity of the Lord Jesus. This word is only used to describe deity. Second, it is used to describe a surprise appearance. This describes the coming of the Lord!

The idea is, "Listen, Buddy, you'd better be doing this right. You'd better be serious about your oath, because the Lord Jesus Christ is going to come, and it's going to be a surprise appearance! Would you be ready if He appeared today? Would He find you faithful to the oath you have taken?"

Now why does Paul say this to Timothy? He is again laying emphasis on the responsibility Timothy has received in the Lord. He cannot mess up this call. He cannot take his ministry lightly, because Jesus is going to come. It's going to be a surprise appearance, and Timothy is going to answer for that oath that he made before God.

Now look at verse 2, where we see *the oath*. It says, "Preach the word; be instant in season, out of season; reprove, rebuke, exhort with all longsuffering and doctrine." Notice Paul doesn't say, "Work signs and wonders." What does he say? He says, "Preach the Word." Do you know why?

If you build a foundation on the Word, signs and wonders will follow. They will *follow,* but they will not *precede.* So he says, "Preach the word...."

God's Imperial Heralds!

Now pay careful attention to the word "preach." This is the Greek word *keruxon.* This was not originally a Christian word at all. This word "preach" *(keruxon)* was the Greek word used to describe the spokesman of the emperor. A technical term for him would be *the Imperial Herald* — the man who had access to the throne room.

He would go into the throne room and say, "O king, what is your message for the people?" He would listen to the words of the king, and the king would give him a special message for the people.

He would then leave the throne room of the king and would come out into the streets. A crowd would gather around him, and he would speak on behalf of the king. "Thus saith our king," he would begin — and then he would say exactly what that emperor had said.

This was the most noble position in government. This was the job that everyone wanted, because you had access to the king. And not only that, you were *his* spokesman. You were invested with such power that you could actually speak on *his* behalf. It was most notable. And never, never did an Imperial Herald take his job lightly. He understood that it was a privilege to be a spokesman for the king. What an honor to be the Imperial Herald!

By using this word *keruxon,* Paul says to Timothy, "Timothy, you need to understand the privilege that is attached to the preaching of the Gospel. Don't ever take this lightly. You are the Herald of the King. You have a place in His Throne Room. You go in. You hear what He says, and you and just a few others have the power to go out and speak directly from His throne."

'Preach the Word'

I hope you understand how powerful this word "preach" is. This word "preach" indicates that we should not be sloppy about preaching.

First, it means we need to *know the message.*

If I was going to go in to the President, and he was going to give me a message, how would I take that message? Would I take it lightly, or would I memorize it? I would memorize it. I would *know the message.*

Second, I would *speak it with accuracy.*

Third, there is a *solemnness* attached to the call of God.

The pulpit is not a place where you stand up and crack jokes and act like nothing in the world is serious. This doesn't mean you can't have fun in the pulpit; I have fun in my meetings. But I want you to know, we move beyond the fun to the message the Holy Ghost is bringing. Preaching and teaching have eternal ramifications! We need to realize the solemnness attached to preaching and teaching.

Fourth, you must understand there is a *responsibility* inherent in the call.

Many people come to me and say, "Hey, how did your ministry get started? You know, it looks like fun. You get to travel — you get to go to the mountains and the ocean, and it's probably great money!" Saints, there is a great responsibility attached to the call of God. It's more than fun. It's serious.

Fifth, we need to understand that the preaching of the Gospel is *a privilege.* It's not a burden. It's not something cumbersome in our life. When we understand the privilege that is attached to this, we will never disdain or hate the ministry. We'll be so thankful that God chose us; that we can go into His Throne Room, hear what He has to say, and step out and speak on His behalf.

So Paul says to Timothy, "Preach the Word. You are the Imperial Herald." Preach the what? "Preach the Word." What

71

we are to major on above all else as preachers of the Gospel is *the Word.*

We are to major on the Word more than we are to major on signs and wonders.

You may ask, "Rick, why do you keep driving that home?" Because signs and wonders will *follow* if we are truly doing the job of an Imperial Herald. Preach the Word. Preach the Word. Preach the Word.

In fact, the Greek language here is in the repetitive sense. It means, "Preach, preach, preach, preach, preach, preach, preach, preach. And after that, keep on preaching some more, keep on preaching some more, keep on preaching some more." Really, the whole idea is, "Give yourself over to this completely. Be devoted to it."

'I Confirm Only My Word'

One day I said, "Lord, we've not had any major signs and wonders for a while. Why?"

He said, "You haven't been preaching my Word. You've told stories. You've made people laugh. But you haven't preached my Word."

He continued, "I never said I'd confirm your stories, your jokes, or your personality. I confirm only my Word."

I understood God wanted me to preach Word, Word, Word.

Now look at verse 2: "Preach the word; be instant in season, out of season; reprove, rebuke, exhort with all longsuffering and doctrine."

What in the world does Paul mean, "be instant"? It's the Greek word *epistemi.* This is a military term which indicates that part of ministry is *warfare.* Did you know that part of ministry is warfare? Really, this phrase "be instant" in the Greek means "stick to your post." Stick to your post! And what is the post of a Gospel preacher? *The pulpit.* We're looking at the ministry of the Word from the pulpit.

So a literal translation would be, "Stick to your post. Stick to your job. *Stay at that pulpit.*" There is a run on the pulpit today; everyone wants to be in the pulpit. That pulpit is one of the most holy places in the Body of Christ.

'Stay at Your Post'

And Paul says to Timothy, "Stay at your post. Stick to the pulpit. You concentrate on what God has called you to do. Don't you dare release it. Don't you dare hand it to another man. It's yours. You stay right there. God gave you that post. You'd better stick to it. You'd better be instant in this thing."

Then notice what else he says: "Be instant in season, out of season. . . ." What does that mean — in the fall and in the spring?" No! This phrase "in season" is the Greek word *eukairos*, which is literally translated, "Stick to your post when times are *good*." What does "out of season" mean? "Stick to your post when times are *bad*." Or, "Timothy, the Word is *always* right, regardless of the season."

Then Paul says what you are to do *from* the pulpit *with* the Word. The Word will do these things. He says: "(1) *Reprove*; (2) *rebuke*; (3) *exhort with all longsuffering.*" Then he mentions the "biggie" — what is it? (4) "*Doctrine.*"

Underline the word "reprove" in your Bible. This word "reprove" is a very powerful Greek word. It means to prove it from the Word.

With the Word, you can bring a sinner to the point of *conviction.* Not necessarily to the point of *confession*; but to the point of conviction.

This scripture is a picture of a man who has become a *channel for the Word.* This preacher/teacher is so powerful in the Word that everyone listening is confronted by God. We need this type of confrontation in the Church today!

It says next: "Reprove and *rebuke.*" This word "rebuke" is a Greek word, *epitimao*, which means to censor or stop something. If you truly give yourself to the Word, the Word flowing through you will have the power *to stop sin* without counseling sessions. The Word itself will issue the rebuke! The Word itself will bring about the adjustment!

The Pastor's Priority

A pastor called me one day. He asked, "Now, Rick, you travel the country and you see all these different churches. What do you think is the most important thing a local pastor can do?"

I said, "Well, I know exactly what it is."

He said, "What is it?"

I answered, "Do a good job in the pulpit. That's your number one responsibility."

He said, "What! That's the *least* thing that I do. I thought you would say, 'Counsel' or, 'Start home cell groups,' because I've got all this free time during the week. I'm in the pulpit just two or three times a week — surely that couldn't be the most important thing."

What does the Bible say? We need to understand that preaching the Word is not just something we do because it's Sunday morning. We need to have been in the Throne Room of the King, heard what His Word was for that morning, and come out as the spokesman of the King, speaking with accuracy, authority, and power.

And if we have come from the Throne Room of the King, *God's Word will issue a censure, a rebuke, and an adjustment.* "Where the word of a king is, there is power. . ." (Ecclesiastes 8:4).

Notice what Paul says next: "Reprove, rebuke, *exhort with all longsuffering and doctrine.*" This word "longsuffering" goes hand in hand with "doctrine." Here's the reason why: If you're going to teach doctrine, you'd better be able to do it with longsuffering.

Today people associate doctrine with *dead denomi-nationalism*. That's what they think doctrine is. I've heard people say, "Don't give us that *doctrine!* We had doctrine when we were in our denominational church. We don't want any doctrine. We're not going to be a doctrine church. We're going to be a 'sweet, loving Jesus, Holy Spirit' church. Don't give us that doctrine."

Teachers Need Longsuffering

But the word "doctrine" is simply the word "teaching." That's all it means. And know this: When you teach people, you had better be able to do it with lots of longsuffering; especially in these last days.

The word "longsuffering" is the Greek word *makrothumia,* from *makros,* which means "long" — that's where we get the word "macaroni" — and from the word *thumia* or *thumos,* which refers to swelling passions or desires. Put the two words together, and they describe a man who has the ability to burn for a long, long time.

Why does Paul say you've got to walk in longsuffering if you teach doctrine? Because people eventually say to themselves, "If my pastor teaches on that doctrine one more time, I won't know what I'm going to do! He has been in the Gospel of John for two years!" (People have a way of getting tired of hearing good doctrine!) Honestly, if you really did a good job with the Gospel of John, you could stay in it five years. You can't get enough of good doctrine.

People have a way of saying, "Come on — give me some razzle-dazzle! I've heard this before." Do you know what they really mean? "We don't like foundation. Let's just build the house. We want to go straight to the attic. Would it be O.K. if we ignored this foundation stuff?" However, if you build a house without a foundation, it will not last very long.

Castles in the Clouds

I'll never forget the vision I had when I was first called into the ministry. I saw a giant castle — a beautiful edifice.

75

The Lord spoke to me and said, "Son, I am showing you what most modern-day ministries look like to Me."

I replied, "Lord, it's so fabulous! Lord, it's like a castle. It's like a mansion. Lord, it's like a kingdom."

The Lord said, "Look at the foundation." This castle was sitting way up in the clouds on top of a rickety, old scaffolding. And the Lord said, *"Everything that looks impressive is not."*

We need a foundation. We *must have* a foundation.

Paul now has told Timothy, "Son, I'm going to tell you that when you begin to teach the Word, you'd better do it with longsuffering, because sometimes people are going to get tired of the Word, and you're going to have to be able to work with those people. You're going to have to be able to exhort them. You're going to have to burn for a long, long time. And don't you forget, Timothy, your number one responsibility is *doctrine*."

In verse 3, Paul says, "For the time will come when they will not endure sound doctrine." (We're talking about *today*.) He continues: ". . . but after their own lusts shall they heap to themselves teachers, having itching ears; And they shall turn away their ears from the truth, and shall be turned unto fables. But watch thou in all things, endure afflictions, do the work of an evangelist, make full proof of thy ministry" (vv. 4,5).

Self-Centered Christians

Go back to verse 3, where he says, "For the time will come." That phrase "will come" is from the word *eimi* in the Greek. It means "I am." It describes a self-centered, self-seeking attitude within the Church; a people who are no longer concerned about the Word; no longer concerned about the world — a people who are concerned about themselves and *spiritual entertainment*. (We've got a lot of spiritual entertainment today.)

The chief concern of these people is to have a good time. They don't care about substance. They say, "Don't give me *meat*; give me *cake*." That's what we're talking about.

Now notice the next phrase: "For the time will come when they will not endure sound doctrine...." Especially notice the word "endure," the word "sound," and the word "doctrine."

The word "endure" is the Greek word *anechomai*, which means "to put up with," "to bear with," or "to tolerate." The word "sound" is the Greek word *hugiaino*, which refers to something that is "healthy." Really, a better translation would be, "For the time will come when they will no longer tolerate healthy doctrine."

Again, the word "doctrine" is *didaskalia*, which means "good teaching." So a literal translation would be, "For a self-centered time will develop in the Church when they will no longer tolerate food that is good for them."

Lack of Foundation, Lack of Discernment

If I placed a can of poison in front of you and said, "Eat this," would you eat it? Of course not. Why? Because you know that it's poison. Do you know what the Bible is teaching here? The Bible is teaching that in *the last* of the last days, there is going to be such a *lack of foundation* that people won't know enough of the Word to discern what's good and what's bad. Therefore, they'll eat anything that's put in front of them. *Anything!*

One man has translated it: "For a time will come when they will not hold themselves back from bad food." This conveys the right idea accurately.

Paul continues in verse 3, "For the time will come when they will not endure sound doctrine; but after their own lusts shall they heap to themselves teachers, having itching ears."

The word "lusts" describes the condition of their heart. God will give you the desire of your heart — whether your desire is right or wrong.

77

This word "lusts" is the Greek word *epithumia*, which refers to strong, strong desire. So this is not a passing fancy, but a deep-rooted desire. It describes people who are doubled over with a strong passion.

The Bible teaches here that in the last days, people won't want sound doctrine. They will want something "frilly." This will be the cry of their heart: "We want something *exciting!* Give us something never heard before!"

As I travel the country, there are times when the Lord won't let me flow in the gifts of the Holy Ghost. Do you know why? Because people say, "Don't give us the Word. We want a word of knowledge!"

There are times when I've heard the Lord say, "Son, I'm sorry, but I'm not going to do it. Don't ask Me, because I'm not going to. I'm not giving them *cake* when they haven't even had *meat.*"

The Pull To 'Perform'

There is a pull on the preacher today to "perform." Nearly every service I go into these days, I am confronted with this decision, because I feel a pull from the people: "Tell us stories. Tickle our ears. Give us something we've never heard before, because we're tired of the regular Word."

And the people are giving birth to the kind of teachers they want. Do you know there are some people who will give you what you want? If you want a story, they'll give you one. If you want a tale, some people will give you one. And the Bible says this is a last-days phenomena that will occur inside the Church. (It should make you grateful if you're part of a *good* church.)

Understand, it's not wrong to tell stories in order to build faith, or to make a point; the Bible is full of stories. However, we must have "meat" along with those stories. *Signs and wonders don't follow funny stories. They follow the Word!*

"....they shall heap to themselves teachers, having itching ears." This does not refer to the teachers; rather, this refers to the people. This phrase "itching ears" refers to a strange curiosity for new tidbits of information on the part of the people. In fact, it is "an insatiable curiosity."

These are the people who will go from meeting to meeting to meeting, looking for some new type of enlightenment; something that's a brand-new revelation. They have an incredible, inordinate passion for spicy tidbits of revelation. Oh, they get all these new "words from God"!

Did you know that crazy teaching didn't happen a hundred years ago? It didn't. It didn't happen 50 years ago, either, because there was so much sound teaching in the Church. But today there is such a lack of good teaching that people have floated out into *realms of silliness.*

'Who Wants To Give Birth?'

A friend of mine went to a prayer meeting like this. Someone was teaching and said, "Now it's time to give birth in the Spirit." (I believe that some things are birthed in the Spirit, and I have birthed some things in the Spirit, but women don't have babies every day, and they're glad about it!)

The woman doing the teaching said, "Who wants to give birth tonight?" A young lady said, "I do." So this young lady lay down on the floor, and the teacher said, "Now we need some spiritual midwives." Two ladies volunteered.

The young lady on the floor began pushing and groaning, while one lady prayed in tongues and rubbed her body and the other lady prayed in tongues and sat between her legs to "catch." (We're talking about genuine, spiritual freaks!)

But do you know what's wild? *The stranger the teaching, the more people think that it's of God!* The stranger and the wilder it is, the quicker people are to believe it! Do you know why? They have *no foundation.* If they had a foundation of the Word, discernment would be working in their life. But because there is no foundation in their life, they say, "Gosh, that sounds exciting! Can *I* give birth the next time?" And they think that this practice is all right.

Immature people view this as true spirituality. It is pure foolishness — that's what it is. Why? Because there's *no foundation* in their lives. Therefore, these immature people have nothing by which to judge whether it's right or wrong.

They'll "eat" anything you put in front of them if you'll put the label of "God" on it. Just give it to them. They want it. Give them some more! And all the while, it's producing error in their life.

The Itching Ears Syndrome

Now look what it says next: ". . .having itching ears." Again, this describes the people who say, "Give me more. Give me more. Give me more! I have a curiosity that desires to know more. Give me more! Give me more!"

Verse 4 says, ". . .they shall turn away their ears from the truth." This means they had the truth, but they turned from the truth. That is why First Timothy chapter 4 verse 1 says, "Now the Spirit speaketh expressly that in the last times some shall *depart from*. . . ." And you see here in Second Timothy 4:4 it says, "They shall 'turn away.' "

This word "turn away" again is a Greek word which indicates a radical character change. The idea is, a mass character change will occur within the Church in the last days. Silliness will replace seriousness. This is a prediction that people en masse will begin accepting strange teachings that just 10 years earlier would never have been accepted.

As I travel and talk with pastors, they confirm this is happening. A great frustration for pastors today is dealing with all the absolutely foolish teaching that is going around. For some pastors, this consumes nearly all their time — putting one fire out after another — just in time to find another new one that needs to be put out.

The difficulty of this becomes apparent when the people in error think the pastor is unspiritual. They say to him, "Pastor, you're missing this new move of God. You're the one who's wrong, pastor, not us. We have a new revelation!"

Recently, one pastor asked me, "Is it like this all over the country?" You see, it seems there has been a character change in the Church in the past years. This radical change has touched every part of the nation.

'Bones' Out of Joint

"They shall slowly turn away their ears from the truth and shall be turned unto fables." Now look at the phrase "turned unto." This is a medical word. This is the Greek word *ektrepomai*. It refers to a bone that is out of joint. This means these deceived people are still saved, but they are out of joint with the rest of the Church. Or they are out of joint with the rest of solid Christian teaching.

What happens when you have a bone in your body that's out of joint? It hurts, doesn't it? In fact, when a bone is out of joint, it hinders the movement of the entire body. It slows activity down. It hinders development. And when error is in the Church, it hurts the Church.

Now notice what else it says: "They shall be turned unto fables." "Fables" is the Greek word *muthos*, which really is the word "mythology."

Turn to First Timothy chapter 1 verse 3 to see an example of fables in the Church. This problem of false teaching and wrong teaching has been in the Church from its inception. But the Bible says it's going to culminate in the last days, and it's going to be *far* worse than it's ever been. It's going to all start happening at once. It's happening *right now*.

How the Word Movement Is Splitting

There are two groups forming now: the *Power Group* and the *Word Group*. The Power Group says the Word Group is boring, and the Word Group says the Power Group doesn't have any foundation.

There needs to be a coming together of the two. I'm one man who wants to be a part of *both* groups. I want to channel the Holy Ghost, *and* I want to channel the Word!

However, I'm going to start with the foundation. You'll never hear from these lips that the day of the Word or teaching is over. Never! That day will never be over. Never!

Look here again and see what it says in First Timothy 1:3,4: "As I besought thee to abide still at Ephesus, when I went into Macedonia, that thou mightest charge some that they teach no other doctrine. Neither give heed to fables and endless genealogies, which minister questions, rather than godly edifying which is in faith."

You can always count on it: if teaching is wrong — if they're feeding you "cake" and not "meat" — it will just lead to another question. It will never give you substance. It will never fulfill you. You will be on an endless train of thought — ever learning, but never able to come to recognition of the truth. You will go from one thing to another, and then another thing to another thing, because it will never bring you satisfaction.

First Century Know-It-Alls

But notice what these saints were into: "fables and endless genealogies." The key here is the phrase "endless genealogies." The Greek could be translated, "unbelievably, far-stretched research." The idea is "exaggeration" — brains that have gone off track. They are deluded; they are imagining things. This research has no substance and no foundation to it. This is describing Gnostics.

The word "Gnostic" is from *gnosis*, which means "I know." We still have that group today. We have that group in the Word Movement. They are the Gnostics; they have superior intelligence, special light that no one else has. They've been where no man has been. They've gone beyond the veil, and they know special revelation. We're talking about modern-day Gnosticism. It's in the Church today.

Second Timothy 4:4 continues, "And they shall turn away their ears from the truth, and shall be turned unto fables." Again, this phrase "shall be turned" means they become like a dislocated bone.

They are still in the body, but they are dislocated from the rest of the body. They are out of joint. Yes, they're saved. Yes, they're part of the Church. Yes, they're going to heaven. And, yes, they're still called of God. But they are *dislocated*, and they are causing a tremendous problem. They need to repent and be snapped back into place. We need a Holy Ghost adjustment today!

Paul's Advice to Preachers

In verse 5, Paul begins to speak directly to Timothy *and to every preacher* or minister of the Gospel. He says, "But watch thou in all things, endure afflictions, do the work of an evangelist, make full proof of thy ministry."

Command number one: "Watch thou in all things."

Command number two: "Endure afflictions."

Command number three: "Do the work of an evangelist."

Command number four: "Make full proof of thy ministry."

The first phrase, "watch thou," is the Greek word *nephe*, actually from *nepho*, which refers to a man who is sober. You could translate it, "Do not become intoxicated like the rest." Or, even better, "Stay sober." I like to translate it like this: "Stay straight."

Why does Paul tell Timothy, "Stay straight"? He's talking about Timothy's preaching. He's talking about Timothy's doctrine. He's talking about the way Timothy is thinking.

Why does Paul say to Timothy, "Timothy, stay straight. Stay sober. Don't get intoxicated"? Because Timothy is surrounded by all kinds of strange doctrines. Everywhere he looks, he's hearing something new that's exceedingly flaky. It's unbelievable. And do you know what? Everyone believes it but him!

Every day, Timothy hears something spectacular, sensational, and unbelievable — something out of the realm of the spirit. The next day he hears something else. He's noticing how the people are responding to it; how they're "eating it up." They're saying, "Give me more. Give me more. Give me more!"

Do you know what Timothy is tempted to think? "Maybe they're all right and I'm wrong. I'm the only one who seems to think this way. All these other people are coming up with these doctrines that have never been heard before. Maybe they're the ones who are spiritual. Maybe I'm the one who's unspiritual and carnal."

This word *nepho* also means to be vigilant and aware of all the events taking place around you — yet, proceeding on your already established course with calmness and steadiness. In other words, don't be moved by all you hear and see!

How To Handle the Sensational

I deal with this all the time! I see all the new books that come out and sell as fast as candy. I hear all these new things. The people currently are talking about — *angel oil!* They come up to me in my meetings and say, "Brother Renner, have you heard about the angel oil?"

"No, I haven't."

"Look at my Bible. See that huge smudge all over the page? See how all the ink has been faded, and it bled into the margin? See it? *An angel* did that in a meeting the other night. It's *angel oil!* Smell it."

One man came up to me and said, "My Bible was zipped up in my Bible case, and the angel oil got inside the

Bible case. Look at my Bible — I can't even use it anymore. Do you see the oil?"

Everyone's talking about it. It's the talk of the people in some areas of the nation. These people are so captivated, do you know what it made me want to do? Have angel oil in *my* meetings! "There must be something wrong," I thought. "I don't understand — if this is the new move, Lord, why aren't people's Bibles being smudged with grease during *my* meetings?"

I tell you, there are times I have to shake myself and say, "This is not right. I do not have to do this." The devil says to me, "You're just carnal. You're just unspiritual. You don't have any signs and wonders. Your problem is, you're just a Word man. Old, boring Word! You need to throw that Word out and drip blood and drip oil."

At such times, I have to shake myself and say, "Heaven and earth shall pass away, but my word shall abide forever." "Where the word of a king is, there is power." "Not one jot, not one tittle shall pass away." "My word abides forever." "I have exalted my word above my own name." It's like I have to shake myself and say, "Renner, stay straight!"

Don't Throw the Baby Out

Do you know what we've got to watch out for? We've got to watch out that we don't throw the baby out with the bath water — that we don't throw the whole thing out.

There *is* a genuine move of the Holy Ghost. There are *genuine* manifestations — sometimes *even oil*. But we must build our ministry not on oil, and not on sensationalism, but on the Word.

I know you're tired of "show biz" ministry. I'm tired of it, too. I'm tired of people who are *supposed* to be healed, but aren't. We're all hungry for a genuine encounter with God, aren't we? That's what I want. I want signs and wonders!

We all want to see the glory of God, and we've been building a foundation for that glory to roll in upon. Aren't you excited about that? The glory of God never filled the Temple until the house was built first. I think we sometimes get ahead of things.

So Paul's first command was, "Watch thou in all things. Stay straight. Keep your head on. Don't get drunk like the rest."

His second command was, "Endure afflictions." Now why does he say, "Endure afflictions?" If you're the only one thinking the way you're thinking — if you're in the minority — everyone's opinion might be against you. And what Paul is saying is, "Timothy, it doesn't matter how much silliness is going on around you; you endure because you know you've been in the Throne Room of the King. You've heard what the King has to say. You don't need the opinions of others. You don't need the approval of others. You've been in the Throne Room. What else do you need?"

When you know you've been with the King, you don't need the approval of anyone else, because you know you have *His* approval. That's why Paul says, "...endure afflictions, do the work of an evangelist."

The Real Meaning of 'Evangelist'

We started this chapter by talking about channelers and mediums. Do you know what the word "evangelist" means in the very oldest sense? It was not a Christian term at all. It was used long before there ever was a Christian Church. It was first found on a non-Christian inscription on a tomb.

The word "evangelist" is actually the word "oracle"!

This means the minister's chief responsibility is to be an "oracle" for God. Of course, this again supports the idea of an Imperial Herald. *We are called to be the Oracle of God.* A technical definition of the word "oracle" would be: (1) A place where deities were consulted, or (2) supernatural knowledge delivered through a medium or priest." An oracle, then, is a conduit of a deity — he is a "channel."

This adds quite a new understanding to the word "evangelist," doesn't it? When Paul says, "Do the work of an evangelist," in reality he is saying, "Become the best channel of the Holy Ghost you can be. Learn to yield to the Spirit. Yield to the Word. Timothy, you must develop yourself into an excellent channel for God's Word. Become His oracle."

In this sense, all ministers are evangelists. We are all called to be His mouthpiece.

Then Paul continues in verse 5, ". . . make full proof of thy ministry." This, too, is a tremendously misunderstood statement. What does "full proof" refer to? Is it signs and wonders? No, not in this sense.

This phrase "make full proof" is the Greek word for "fullness" or "completion." A better translation would be "Bring your ministry to fullness." Or, "Develop your ministry — working harder all the time to make it the best it can be."

Remember, in context Paul is talking about the preaching and teaching of doctrine. So what Paul really is saying is, "Work hard at becoming the oracle of the Word — and never stop until you have made your ministry the best it can be."

Good teachers and preachers aren't made by accident. In the next chapter, we will see how to become a good minister of Jesus Christ in these perilous times.

Rick Renner's Expanded Translation of Second Timothy 4:1-5
(Freely Translated)

Knowing what I am about to say will summon the full attention of God, I now with great seriousness and solemnness give you this important charge. Understand that the eyes of God and the Lord Jesus Christ are right now fixed on you. God's gaze is set — He is watching to see how seriously you take this command, and He will continue watching to see if you will fulfill it. Soon the Lord Himself will come to make a crucial examination, not only of the dead, but also of the living. This, Timothy, includes you — this examination of your life and commitment will occur when you least expect it, and He will do it with the full backing of His kingdom.

Preach the Word as the Imperial Herald of the King — speak His message accurately, adding nothing to it, and taking nothing away from it. You have been given a privilege and an important position, so herald His Word exactly as it was first spoken to you by Him. This is your chief responsibility. Be on standby, ready at any moment to hear what the King has to say, and never, never, never leave your post. If necessary, speak His Word even if it results in warfare. Regardless of your situation, never relinquish that pulpit God has given you. This is your post and yours alone; stay there when times are good and enjoyable, and stay there when times are bad and difficult. With this Word you must bring offenders to a place of conviction. You must preach with such authority that sin is rebuked and stopped. You must do this important work of exhortation with longsuffering — patiently working with the people and constantly giving them doctrine: excellent, clear teaching that they can understand.

Because a strange season of selfishness and foolish immaturity will come when they will no longer tolerate sound, solid, healthy doctrine — though they need the sound teaching of scripture — they will slowly begin to reject it. Like a child, they will push away meats that are good for them and will take excesses into their lives that eventually will have the effect of poison. After a time, they will devour any spiritual substance placed in front of them, without discerning whether it's good or bad. After their own lusts shall they heap to themselves pile on top of pile of their own favorite teachers. These teachers will not come with a real Word of God; rather, with tidbits of new, spicy revelation to satisfy their abnormal curiosity for new ideas and new teachings.

And they will slowly begin to change — it will seem as though their character is being transformed right in front of you. The effect of unhealthy teaching will blur their thinking, and they will turn their ears from the truth and shall be turned unto fables. While they pursue this wrong way of thinking, they will become like a dislocated bone in the Body — still a part of the Church, but disjointed and a cause for genuine irritation and pain for others. While they pursue error, the rest of the Body is hurt. Just as a dislocated bone restricts movement, they will hinder the real development of the Church.

So Timothy, keep your head on straight. Don't be influenced, overwhelmed, and intoxicated by all the error around you. Rather, maintain a steady, calm course in all things, and especially in your teaching. You must determine to stand your ground and know you will be misunderstood. Your steady, calm course may become the subject of scorn and lack of appreciation; however, your chief responsibility is to be the Lord's spokesman. Regardless of what others say and teach, you speak only what you have heard the Lord say to you — and, Timothy, it is your responsibility to take your ministry and your gift as far as you can take it. Therefore, carry your ministry out into the fullest expression possible.

Chapter 6
Ministering in the Last Days

Where there is no foundation of the Word, you are in a position to be seduced by doctrines of devils.

I'm seeing this happen all across the United States. People today basically do not have a foundation of good doctrine in their lives. And the Bible says because of that, they won't know if it's good spiritual food or bad food they are consuming. They will turn their ears away from a healthy teaching and will be turned rather unto fables.

With this in mind, look at First Timothy chapter 4 verse 6. Paul says to Timothy:

> **If thou put the brethren in remembrance of these things, thou shalt be a good minister of Jesus Christ, nourished up in the words of faith and of good doctrine, whereunto thou hast attained.**
>
> **But refuse profane and old wives' fables, and exercise thyself rather unto godliness.**
>
> **For bodily exercise profiteth little: but godliness is profitable unto all things, having promise of the life that now is, and of that which is to come.**
>
> **1 Timothy 4:6-8**

For the sake of review, I want to remind you of this first phrase, "If thou put the brethren in remembrance...." This is one of the poorest translations in the entire New Testament, because the Greek word here is the word *hupotithemi.*

Building a Firm Foundation

This word *hupotithemi* should be translated, "if you build a firm foundation under the brethren." Paul's talking about building a firm foundation.

Hupo means "underneath," and *tithemi* means "to place, or to lay a foundation." So rather than putting the brethren in remembrance, Paul says, "If you want to be a good minister of Jesus Christ, then you must be a minister who builds a foundation underneath them."

You could translate it, *"If you build a firm foundation under the brethren,* thou shalt be a good minister of Jesus Christ, nourished up in the words of faith and of good teaching, whereunto thou hast attained."

Notice that phrase "good minister." The word "good" is the Greek word *kalos.* This tells us God's opinion of a man who builds a firm foundation. This word *kalos* is how God describes a minister who takes care and time to develop his people and to lay a foundation of the Word underneath his people.

The word *kalos* means "beautiful, virtuous, delightful, well-pleasing." This is the kind of ministry gift that we desire to be, whether we are in the pulpit ministry, the music ministry, or any form of ministry. We want to be found of the Lord to be beautiful, delightful, pleasing, and virtuous. And the Bible says God takes delight in a man or a woman who takes time to build a foundation underneath the Church.

Slaving for the Kingdom

Notice what it says next: "If you build a firm foundation under the brethren, you will be a good, wonderful, beautiful, delightful *minister* of Jesus Christ." This word "minister" is the Greek word *diakonos. Diakonos* is the same word for the word "deacon" in Acts 6:2. This means the minister is, above all other things, a *deacon.* He is a *servant!*

Today we talk a great deal about ministry and about being ministers, but the word "ministry" is just a glorified term for a slave or a servant! We will never build a foundation under the Church — we will never build a foundation of the Word under the people — until we come to grips with the fact that we are not called to be a glorified star.

Rather, we are the servant of all. God has called us to be the chief deacons in the Church. And the only way we will ever build a foundation under the Church is if we pour our life out into those people. We can't do this only on Sunday. We can't do this just with a special meeting. This word *diakonos* indicates this is going to require every fiber of our spirit, our soul, and our body.

Ministries are crumbling all around us. Satan has done a lot of it. But, praise the Lord, God is working some good out of it! Through it all, God is reminding us about the importance of the local church. He's reminding us that Jesus gave His life for it, and we need to be committed to it, regardless of the cost.

Jesus: Our Example

Paul continues, ". . .thou shalt be a good minister of Jesus Christ." Circle that word "of," and take special notice of it. You could translate it, "Thou shalt be a good minister *'like'* Jesus Christ."

The idea is, Jesus is our example of the Chief Deacon. Jesus said, ". . .whosoever will be great among you, let him be your minister [*diakonos*, the deacon, the servant of all]; And whosoever will be chief among you, let him be your servant: Even as the Son of man came not to be ministered unto, but to minister. . ." (Matthew 20:26-28).

Again, this word "ministry" implies that those who are called into full-time work are the public officials and the public servants of the Church. If you want to know what kind of opinion we should have of ourselves, or why we must recognize the gift of God in us, we should not see ourselves as a glorified star who is untouchable. Rather, we are called to be the servants of the Church.

And let me tell you, when we recognize that we are the servants of the Church, our feelings won't get hurt quite so often. It's when we think we're so special, so holy, and so anointed that we ask, "Why don't they treat me like I'm special?"

Now, don't misunderstand me: Ministry gifts *should* be honored — but they should not be worshipped. They *should* be honored. They *should* be *very* honored. However, they had hero infatuation in the city of Corinth. That's one reason the city of Corinth was so divided.

One group followed Paul, another group followed Peter, another group followed Apollos, and another group said they followed Christ. The "Christ" group was the worst of all, because they were the superspirituals.

Have you ever run into this group? The "Christ" group can submit to no one and follow no one but Christ. That's the worst crowd of all. Often their attitude is disguised rebellion!

How should we think of ministry gifts? In First Corinthians 4:1, Paul says, "Let a man so account of us, as of the ministers of Christ, and stewards of the mysteries of God." This is the way we are to think of ministry gifts.

Row, Row, Row Your Boat

The word "account" is the Greek word *logidzomai*, which means "reckon us like this," or "think of us like this." Paul says, "We are the ministers of Christ." This word "ministers" used in First Corinthians 4:1 refers to the men who were in the bottom of a ship, rowing the boat.

These were not the men on the deck. These were the men in the bottom of the boat. This was *slave labor!* These were the men who were doing all the rowing, all the oaring, pouring out all of their energies in order to move that boat.

And Paul says, "If you need to know what to think about me, you need to understand I'm the *slave* in the bottom of the boat who keeps the ship moving. You're up on top, enjoying the ride, and here I am in the bottom, rowing, rowing, and rowing."

He says, "I'm pouring my whole life out in order that the Church will move, grow, and excel."

If you're going to do good ministry, it's going to require much of you. The Church cannot be developed by ministers with a lazy attitude. You must give yourself to your ministry in order to see the Church mature, grow, and move with God. Fivefold ministry gifts *should* be honored because of their hard work and valuable position.

In First Timothy chapter 4 verse 6, Paul says, "If thou put the brethren in remembrance of these things...," or "If you build a firm foundation under the brethren...you will be a good, delightful, beautiful, wonderful servant, just like Jesus Christ."

Nourished by the Word

Now look at what Paul says next: "...nourished up in the words of faith and of good doctrine, whereunto thou hast attained." Notice the phrase "nourished up." This Greek word, *entrepho,* means "to eat something, to digest it, and incorporate it into your system."

What you find is, no one *in their flesh* is going to pour their life out for the Church. No one wants to be *the servant* of all — *unless* they are nourished up in the words of faith and of good doctrine.

Paul says, "The reason you are willing to pour your life out is because of what the Word has done in your life." He's talking about the power of the Word — the Word creates within us a servant mentality.

And Paul specifically mentions two things which Timothy has eaten, digested, and incorporated. He says, "You have eaten, you have digested, you have incorporated into your life the *words of faith* and of *good doctrine."* These are two areas that we must never get away from. We can never get enough of faith — *never!* And we can never get enough good doctrine!

We're part of a Word Movement and a Faith Movement. Sometimes it seems we know everything there is to know about faith, but we do not. We can never get away from faith. In fact, *if we get away from faith, we're going to lose the supernatural element within the Church.*

And Paul says, "Number one, you need to eat on words of faith." He says, "Number two, you need to eat on good doctrine." Most people equate doctrine with dead denominationalism. But the word "doctrine" is the Greek word *didaskalia. Didasko* means "I teach," and *kalia* is from *kalos*, which means "good" or "beautiful." So this phrase "good doctrine" refers to excellent teaching.

Faith and excellent teaching nourish us. They do something in us. They create within us a mentality which makes us willing to *serve;* willing to pour out our life as the Chief Deacon of the Church did.

The Effect of Faith

Then notice what Paul says: "...whereunto thou hast attained." This word "attained" is actually the Greek word *parakoloutheo*, which means, "This is the very thing you have been seeking to become."

How many of you have been seeking to be a good minister of Jesus Christ? This is the thing we're trying to become. Actually, this Greek word *parakoloutheo* (attained) means "to follow with a view to duplicate."

And the idea is, "Timothy, this type of servant is the very thing you've been wishing you could become. You've been imitating me. You've been imitating Christ. This is the very thing, Timothy, you've wanted to be. You wanted to be found of the Lord as a good, faithful, beautiful servant of the Church."

He says, "Timothy, it is the words of faith and of good doctrine incorporated into your life that will make you into this kind of a servant." So we see the power of the Word and the effect of faith in our lives.

In verse 7, Paul says, "But refuse profane and old wives' fables, and exercise thyself rather unto godliness." Well, what do old wives' fables have to do with becoming a good servant of Jesus Christ? Why are old wives' fables so bad, and what is an old wives' fable?

First, notice Paul's opinion of old wives' fables. He says, "But refuse profane and old wives' fables, and exercise thyself rather unto godliness." Underline that word "refuse." This is one of the strongest statements you can make in the Greek. Rather than "refuse," it means "reject, throw out, get rid of, abhor it." The idea is, you need to turn from this with horror, because it will produce something bad in you if you listen to it. Therefore, reject it!

Now Paul gives us his opinion about these fables. He uses the word "profane," the Greek word *bebelos,* which refers to something that is worthless and no good. In fact, it is to be thrown out into the street and to be tramped upon. In other places, it is translated as the word "manure."

So Paul says, "If you want to know what I think about these old wives' fables — as far as I'm concerned, they're dung. They're manure. They stink. They're going to cause a real mess in your ministry."

Some Bad Advice

What does "old wives' fables" refer to here? This specifically referred to the old women who looked at the younger men and said, "Now listen, you're a young person. You've got your whole life ahead of you. I'm older, so listen to wisdom. It would be all right for you to slow down.

"There is no need for you to pour yourself out the way you're doing. You're going to cause yourself to have an ulcer. You're going to have a nervous breakdown. Now, God will understand if you back up just a little bit. He is not going to hold it against you. He doesn't want you to work so hard."

This is an old wives' fable. What did Paul say to do with it? Reject it! Why does he say so strongly to refuse it? Because if you develop that mentality, you'll never build a firm foundation under the Church.

If you have a "take-it-easy, let's-take-our-time, let's-have-fun-along-the-way, let's-not-be-too-serious" mentality, you're never going to be the public servant of Jesus Christ. It is not possible to do so.

Paul says, "Therefore, you must refuse this. You must reject it." The whole idea is, "This is poison, and if this poison gets into your system, it will corrupt you. You will not be able to fulfill the call of God on your life if you have a slothful, lazy mentality."

So Paul says, "Don't listen to those old women. What they are saying is profane. It is dung. It is worthless. Refuse what they are saying to you." Then he says immediately, "Rather, exercise thyself unto godliness."

This word "exercise" is the Greek word *gumnadzo*. The word *gumnadzo* means to exercise while naked. It refers to someone who is stark naked and who is exercising with all his might. It refers to the professional athlete, the man who is so devoted to development that he has said, "I can't even wear clothes when I exercise, because clothes restrict my movement."

So what you find here is Paul saying to Timothy, "You need to have *a devotion to development*." The whole idea is, your ministry will never be developed, and that gift in you will never grow, unless you become *devoted to development*.

Remove All Hindrances

The gift of God doesn't just spring forth by itself. You've got to yield yourself to it. You've got to exercise yourself with it. And Paul says it is essential for you to strip off anything that would hinder you.

This is not a time to take it easy. This is, rather, a time to take off all the restrictions — any hindering things — that would impede you and give yourself to development.

"...exercise thyself unto godliness..." This word "godliness" is the Greek word *eusebeia*. This word *eusebeia* can be translated "piety" or "godliness." But really, both of these ideas miss the mark, because this word *eusebeia* refers to one's loyalty to his religion.

This is what we would call a fanatic — someone who is so deeply devoted to what he is doing that he appears to be fanatical. He is deeply, deeply devoted.

So Paul says, "The way to become more committed — the way to become more developed — is not to sit back and listen to the old women of the church who say, 'Take it easy.' Rather, if you want to be the best you can be, you must give yourself wholly to your ministry. You've got to exercise yourself unto godliness."

And the whole idea of this word *gumnadzo* — "exercise while naked" — is, "There are some things which are keeping you from developing as quickly as you can. And you need to take off these hindering forces so you will have greater movement and you can develop faster."

House-Cleaning Time

There are some things we can do in order to advance our development. For example, there are some things in our lives we need to get rid of! Do you know of anything in your life that you need to get rid of? The Holy Ghost has spoken to me. Has He spoken to you?

We might say, "Lord, I'll deal with that someday, but not now." The Lord's answer? "Fine, but you're the one missing the blessing, because you could be developing right now."

We need to take off these things. We need to minister as freely as we can. We need to give ourselves completely to our gift. In doing so, we will become the best that we can become.

So Paul says, "You're not going to build a firm foundation under the Church unless you do this."

In verse 8, he says, "For bodily exercise profiteth little." Notice two words: the word "profiteth" and the word "little." First of all, he says that bodily exercise *does* profit you. This word "profit" is actually the word for "benefit," or "blessing." It will be a blessing to your body.

Also notice the word "little," because this is the Greek word *oligos* It refers to something that is numerically small. This is a reference to the length of your life. I would translate it like this, "Bodily exercise is good, but short-lived."

I recently met a marathon runner. He heard me teach on this text, and he came to me afterward and said, "Boy, have you hit it on the nail!" He said, "Do you know if I don't run every day, I'll lose ground." He said, "I've got to run every day. Every day must be a new challenge to me. I've got to push myself further and further and further and further and further.

"I have given my life to becoming a marathon runner. I eat the right foods. I exercise. I prepare myself mentally. That's what I've done for my body. Are you telling me that's what God wants me to do with my spirit?"

Exercising the Inner Man

I said, "Exactly." In the same way that an athlete works his body, a man who is called into the ministry must work his soul and his spirit. And if he does not, he will not develop.

Just the other day someone said to me, "Renner, you're like a walking history book. You know all these Greek words, and the history behind every one of them." Another person asked me, "How is it that you can put out so many new tape series each year?"

Do you know why? I have made a decision to yield to the gift that's on the inside of me. And that gift wants to expand. It doesn't matter how hard I work; there's always room for more development. That gift is bigger than anything I could ever dream. It's big. It wants to develop.

Those of us who are pastors, apostles, prophets, evangelists, and teachers need to understand that the gift of Christ in our life contains God in it. It is a divine endowment. It is a powerful gift that can never be exhausted or fully experienced. All God needs is a man or a woman who will yield himself to that gift and flow in it. And regardless of how far we've taken it, we can always take it further. We can always take it further!

Notice what Paul says again in verse 8: "For bodily exercise is a blessing for a short-lived time." He continues, "...but godliness...." That word "godliness" is again the Greek word *eusebeia:* "devotion to your religion, commitment, development, one who is committed."

Paul is saying, "Development and deep commitment have a blessing unto all things, having promise of the life that now is, and of that which is to come."

Then in verse 9 he immediately says, "This is a faithful saying and worthy of all acceptation." Verse 9 tells us this is not just a text for ministers; this text applies to *everyone* in the Body of Christ. He says, "This is worthy of all acceptation." This is not just worthy for ministers and fivefold gifts; this is worthy for *all* acceptation.

Spiritual Muscle-Building

In other words, we need to teach the Church, and we need to teach the people under our care that the Gospel will work you; it will develop you.

Because we are Westerners, we think everything should come easy. But when it comes to spiritual development, it doesn't happen that way. An athlete doesn't become developed in his muscles overnight. He's got to give himself to it. Paul says, "In the very same way, you've got to give yourself to your ministry. You've got to give yourself to your gift."

If you're called into the music ministry, it will not develop by your just sitting and waiting for something supernatural to happen. You have got to give yourself to it. It's not going to be pie-in-the-sky.

Someone can lay hands on you — and it's wonderful to have hands laid on you. It's wonderful to have a transference of the anointing. But I'm going to tell you something: The anointing can hit dead meat! If so, it will produce absolutely nothing. You've got to yield to God's call. You've got to work with your gift. You've got to flow with it if you want it to be developed in your life.

Now guess what this means? This means we are individually responsible. It means that when I stand in front of the Lord, the Lord is going to say, "That gift that I put in your life — what did you do with it?"

And I can't say, "Well, I waited on it to pop out of me! I fasted. I waited. You know, Lord, the Bible says 'If it's ministry, let's wait on our ministry.' Lord, I waited and waited and waited. Nothing ever happened. I just kept waiting." You see, we have misunderstood the gift of God. The gift of God *functions* in those who are *exercised* by it.

People say to me, "Rick Renner, how do you keep up with your regimented schedule?" It's called exercise. I'm not afraid of it. You say, "Is it hard at times?" It is very, very hard. You say, "Hey, Renner, haven't you experienced burnout?" At times I thought I was close. But in the end, I have to thank God. Do you know why? It is exercise.

You see, hardship is all in the way that we view it. If this is just a job that you and I are doing, then I tell you, it s very hard, and it is not worth it. But if it is exercise, then every challenge, every new day, is something to develop us more.

That is what Paul says here: "Exercise, exercise, exercise, exercise, exercise! Give yourself completely to this devotion to development."

In verse 10, Paul now gives his own testimony. He says, "For therefore we both labour and suffer reproach, because we trust in the living God, who is the Saviour of all men, specially of those that believe." In this verse, the words "labour" and the phrase "suffer reproach" are important.

Slothfulness in the Body of Christ

Now let me state something right here: I don't mean to tell you that you must go home and work twenty-four hours every day. But I am going to tell you honestly, there is a lot of slothfulness in the Body of Christ.

God has been speaking to me about my own life. He has told me things that I'm supposed to do; things I'm supposed to fulfill that I haven't even touched yet. And, saints, we must give ourselves to these things, or they are not going to get done. The world is not going to be reached unless Christians realize they've got to give themselves to the ministry.

When we look at the First Century Church, we see that this was a church that was committed. Church was not just a Sunday or a Wednesday night experience. It was an everyday, every-minute experience for every individual.

They believed they were called to take the world for Jesus; therefore, their lives reflected that commitment. They were devoted to development. They were devoted to the call of God. They were devoted to the kingdom. That is why these men and women turned the world upside down. And if we are going to affect our world, we've got to make some changes in the Church.

We have been affected by Western mentality that says, "Take it easy." We don't even like to knock on the door. We just push a little button so the door can ring itself. You know, it's too hard on your knuckles.

We also think it's very difficult to lift the garage door: You've got to get out of the car, bend over, and get back in the car. Then you've got to get back out of the car again and put the garage door back down. That's why we invented electric garage door openers.

The American Way of Sloth

Our entire culture reflects slothfulness — did you know that? We call it "the American way of life." Sadly, it *is* the American way of life.

When you go to buy a refrigerator today, what is essential to have? An automatic ice-maker, because we remember the days when the freezer and the refrigerator were made out of metal. When you would go to get the ice tray, it would be bonded to the metal because it also was made out of metal. Do you remember those days?

You'd have to get a knife and chip away the ice in order to get the ice tray out. Finally — victory! You got it out! You reached down and the lever was frozen, so you pulled and pulled and pulled and pulled and — boom! Every one of those cubes was shattered into a million pieces. Or, you took the tray and ran hot water over it, and reduced every piece of ice to a sliver! Remember those days?

So we became more sophisticated, and we developed ice trays that were made out of blue plastic. Oh, what a wonderful invention that was! All you had to do was twist the tray and the ice cubes popped right out. But in time, even plastic trays became too difficult. They cracked without warning.

You'd walk across the kitchen so carefully. Victory! You didn't spill a drop. You'd put the tray in the freezer compartment and turn around, only to find that you had dribbled water all the way across the kitchen floor.

So someone said, "Enough of this! Let the refrigerator make its own ice." Then that became too hard! We still had to open the freezer door, and that was very hard on our muscles. So we put the ice dispenser on the outside of the door. And then, to save energy, we also put the water dispenser on the outside of the door — to save us from walking across the kitchen to the sink.

One day I went with my sister to the grocery store. I was in a hurry. She said, "Oh, look! I think that person's going to back out of that parking space." The parking lot was not that big to start with.

I said, "Ronda, we're short on time. It's not that far. We can park the car and walk. Why don't you just pull in two spots farther away?"

She said, "No, we'll just wait." You know why? She didn't want to walk the width of two cars!

There's something in our mentality today that is slothful. And it has worked its way into the Church. We need to understand that the Church is not like a remote-control television set. You can't sit in your chair, push a button, and get results. You've got to put all of your body into it, all of your mind into it, and all of your spirit into it, or you and your church will not be developed.

Have you experienced the exercise of the Spirit? We're talking about exercise that requires every ounce of your being.

Ministry as Exercise

Paul refers to this exercise in his own life. He says in verse 10, "For therefore we both labour and suffer reproach." The word "labour" is the Greek word *kopos*. This refers to the farmer who is working out in the field in the hottest period of the day. He is digging the soil. He is working extremely hard. The heat is beating down upon his brow. He is sweating profusely. This refers to sweat and tears and hard, hard work. Paul says, "We are working very, very hard."

Then, if you would, take note of the phrase "suffer reproach." This is a Greek word, *agonidzo*. This word *agonidzo* is where we get the word "agony."

Paul says, "If you want to know the truth of the matter, this ministry that God has given me sometimes is hard work. I'm like the farmer out in the heat of the day. The sun is beating down on my brow. It's hot. I'm sweating profusely. I'm working very, very hard." But there was no other farmer to do the job. He did not have a choice.

Paul says, "In fact, sometimes this ministry God has given me is pure agony." *Agonidzo*. And, really, this word *agonidzo* refers to strenuous action or strenuous activity.

But, you see, Paul does not view this as pain in his life. He has made a decision. Every challenge is further development. Every opportunity for ministry is further development. He has made up his mind he is going to view hardship as exercise. He is going to view ministry as exercise. This is another opportunity for him to release that gift on the inside.

In verse 11 he says, "These things command and teach." This tells us that this applies to *everyone*. The word "command" is the Greek word *parangello*. It means "to transmit." These things "transmit." These things "convey." These things "tell."

The idea is, "These things that I have conveyed to you, Timothy, now you need to convey to your people. They need to understand the labor, the development, and the devotion *they* must have to become all *they* can be in God."

Then he says, "command and *teach*." And the word "teach" is in the imperative, yet it also is a participle. It's a command: "These things teach!" And because it is a participle, it means, "Habitually teach. These things teach, teach, teach, teach, teach, teach, and keep on teaching. These things continually, constantly, habitually teach."

The reason why Timothy must continually, constantly, habitually teach these things is because we have a way of trying to forget these things. And Paul says, "You're going to have to tell it to them, tell it to them, tell it to them, and tell it to them again. These things convey. These things transmit. These things teach."

If You Want Strong Holy Spirit Power

If we are serious about a new move of God's power in the Church today, then we must build a strong foundation of God's Word under the brethren. That power must have a place to rest upon — this is why God loves a minister or a church that builds a foundation underneath the brethren.

How wonderful it would be if we could build a nice, big, beautiful foundation — and then invite people to come stand on it. However, foundation laying doesn't happen this way in the Church.

In order to do this vital work of ministry, we must crawl underneath broken lives, broken people, broken dreams, and Satan's destruction in the lives of people. We must prop them up, build a strong support structure underneath them, and lay that foundation under their broken, shattered lives. This will require a real commitment from everyone involved. Rather than ignore this reality, Paul says to Timothy, "Get under the people and put a firm foundation under their lives."

As we prepare for a last-day revival of the Holy Ghost's power, let's do this vital work of preparation. The Word will give us the foundation we need so desperately, and will impart to us a sense of discernment. Discernment is an absolute necessity for us to have in these days when seducing spirits and doctrines of demons are advancing in the Church as well as in the world.

God's Word properly taught with power will equip us for a last-day supernatural confrontation. Regardless of how hard the work or the cost involved, we must pour ourselves into the church during these days to prepare for this great hour of supernatural confrontation and battle!

Chapter 7
Be Thou an Example

Someone said to me, "You know, in my church, we don't do much...we pray a little...we've understood that God is sovereign...God has given us a prophecy that we're going to be a big church. What do you think?"

I said, "I think God's going to have to choose another church."

The man asked, "Why?"

I said, "Because big churches don't happen by accident. They happen because a group of people is committed to taking the Gospel to their city, and not just *taking* it to their city, but *overtaking* the city. They want to take the city."

People who are going to take their city don't just pray a little and wait for the sovereign move of God. They say, "God give us a strategy! Show us how, because we are ready to go after it."

'Let No Man Despise Thy Youth'

Then in First Timothy 4:12-15, Paul begins to speak specifically to Timothy about developing. He says:

> Let no man despise thy youth; but be thou an example of the believers, in word, in conversation, in charity, in spirit, in faith, in purity.
>
> Till I come, give attention to reading, to exhortation, to doctrine.
>
> Neglect not the gift that is in thee, which was given thee by prophecy with the laying on of the hands of the presbytery.

**Meditate upon these things; give thyself wholly
to them; that thy profiting may appear to all.**

Quickly go back to verse 12 and notice the word
"despise." It is the Greek word *kataphroneo*, which means
"to look down upon," or "to disdain."

Paul said, "Let no man despise thy youth." Why were
people looking down on Timothy? When we think of
youthfulness, we think of a teenager or someone very young.
But this word "youthfulness" is the Greek word *neotes*, which
refers to someone between the age of 30 to 40 years old.

In ancient days, you weren't considered worthy of public
office until you hit 40. Your wisdom didn't even count until
you were 40 or 41 years old. Yet it's not that way in the house
of God.

In First Samuel you find that God called a little boy
named Samuel. Samuel was somewhere between 5 and 7
years old when all Israel attested that he was a prophet of
the Lord. (Can you imagine the United States recognizing
a 5 year old as being a prophet of the Lord?)

You see, God is not interested in age. God is interested
in yieldedness. If you will give yourself to the gift, then
you're the one whom God is going to use.

But why did Paul say, "Let no man despise thy youth?"
Because Timothy did not start this church in Ephesus. This
church was already full-blown when Timothy came to
assume the leadership of it. It is believed the church had
been without a pastor for some time, and the elders in the
church had held the church together in the interim.

Now Paul has set Timothy in the church as pastor.
Timothy is somewhere between 30 and 40 years old, and
those elders are apparently older than this. They are a little
offended that a young whippersnapper would come in and
have authority over them.

They disdained Timothy. They frowned upon him. They
probably talked about him: "Did you hear about our church?
We've got a boy for a pastor."

Paul said, "Ignore it. Let no man despise thy yout And, really, this is a command: "Don't you dare be affect by their opinion!" Paul said. "Rather, develop yourself. Rather than being made fun of, rather than being disdained and looked down and frowned upon," he says, "be thou an example."

'Be Becoming! Be Developing!'

"Be thou" is the Greek word *ginomai*, which could be translated "be becoming." You could translate it, "Keep developing. It's not a time for you to succumb to the opinion of others. This is time for you to let that gift loose and develop it. If they're looking at you, then let your gift go. Let it develop. Let them see you change. Be becoming! Be developing! This is a time for you to emerge!"

I don't know about you, but I'm glad God does not want me to be all these six things instantly. I can't become them instantly. No one can. It just like when the Word says, "Be ye doers of the word. . ." (James 1:22).

When I first heard that, it overwhelmed me, because I thought that instantly, overnight, I had to be accountable for all the Word. But the Greek word is *ginomai:* "Be thou *becoming* a doer of the Word. (Start where you are.) It's time to *develop*. It's time to experiment. It's time to let the gift go."

And here Paul says to Timothy, "Be becoming. Be developing." Notice what else he says: ". . .an example of the believers." The word "example" is the word *tupos*. This is where we get the word for "an example," or "a type." Timothy is to be the type. He is to be the one who is imitated. And for this cause, he must be developing.

Why was it so important for Timothy to develop? Because his church was going to be a reflection of his own life. *The church always reflects the leadership — always.*

You can tell what a pastor is like by looking at his congregation. If he is a loving man, it's going to be a loving church. If he is a sloppy man, it's going to be a sloppy church. If he is an arrogant, haughty man, that's what the church is going to be like.

Paul now mentions six areas in which we are to be examples: "in *word,* in *conversation,* in *charity,* in *spirit,* in *faith,* in *purity."*

First, we are to be an example in *word.* Second, in *conversation.* This is actually the word "character." You're to be an example in your language, and you're to be an example in your character. But character doesn't develop overnight! You've got to give yourself to character development.

Then Paul mentions *charity* (or love) and *spirit.* This word "spirit" refers to a humble attitude and a teachable spirit.

Next Paul mentions *faith* and *purity.* This word "faith" refers to the faith of God. The man of God in the local church must set the pace for faith, and he must continue to walk in it. If he lets loose of faith, the congregation is going to let loose of faith.

The Bible says the two things the minister of God must be consumed with are words of faith and of good doctrine. If a man of God lets loose of faith, he'll let loose of healing in his church. The miraculous will begin to disappear. So Paul says, "These are areas you need to watch."

Paul concludes by mentioning *purity.* This is the word *hagneia,* which undoubtedly refers to physical and *mental* purity. This speaks of sexual purity.

So he said, "Timothy, here are the six areas you need to be working on in your personal life all the time: (1) in word, (2) in character, (3) in faith, (4) in love, (5) in spirit, and (6) in purity."

In verse 13 he says, "Till I come, give attendance to reading, to exhortation, and to doctrine." Pay special attention to the phrase "give attendance." Notice, too, the words "reading, exhortation, and doctrine."

Paul's Formula for Success

I know that those of you who are called of God to teach
and to preach want to be the very best that you can be. And
what you find in verse 13 is Paul giving Timothy a formula
for successfully developing his preaching, teaching gift.

This word "attendance" is the Greek word *proseche*. This
word means "to constantly, habitually give your attendance
to something." Really, it is the very same phrase "be consumed with."

This is a person who eats, drinks, breathes, and sleeps
something. It's on his mind all the time. During his waking
hours, he's thinking about it. He wakes up in the middle
of the night thinking about it. This man constantly has
something on his mind.

We would say this person is a workaholic, or someone
who is so committed he can't do anything else. It's constantly
burning on his or her mind. Even when he's on vacation,
somehow or other it keeps returning to his thoughts. If he's
on an airplane, it comes into his thoughts. If he's talking
to his spouse, it's on his thoughts. This is a person who is
consumed!

If you want your gift to develop, you've got to give
yourself to your gift. If it's a music gift, you've got to give
yourself to it. If prophetic, you've got to give yourself to it.

There's no such thing as a professional prophet. There's
no such thing as a prophet who just prophesies in church
services. Prophets prophesy in bed. They prophesy in the
shower. They prophesy in the kitchen. Prophets will drive
you nuts. They're constantly seeing something — if they're
yielded to their gift.

Success in the Pulpit

Here's the formula: Paul says, "Constantly be consumed
with reading." This word "reading" refers to private reading
of scripture. If you want to be good in the pulpit, first of
all, you've got to have the Word in your own private life.

Don't study it just to preach it. Study it because you want to study it. Study it because you are committed to it.

Notice what Paul said next: "...to exhortation." The word "exhortation" is the Greek word *parakaleo,* which always describes a relationship. It's the same word used to describe the Holy Spirit, the "one who is called *alongside.*" This word "exhortation" in this sense literally means, "when you are attached to the side of someone else, as in relationship with a dear friend." That's the time to talk the Word.

Here's the formula: (1) Read the Word for yourself; (2) let that Word flow out of your life into your closest relationships; into those to whom you are attached.

The Word should be the conversation you have with your friends. The Word should be on your lips. Remember, the word "attendance" means "be consumed with, give yourself to it, habitually, constantly be taken over by it — in your private life and in a circle of friends."

Third, you must give attendance "to doctrine." This word is *didaskalia.* It refers to the public teaching of the Word.

If you want the Word to be powerful in the pulpit, then it's got to be powerful in your private life, and it's got to be powerful in that circle of friends with whom you associate. Anything that happens in the pulpit is simply going to be an overflow of what has already happened in those other two areas. And if it's not happening in those other two areas, then you're going to have a real fizzle in the pulpit. That is what Paul's saying.

It's not hard to know when people don't worship God in their private life, because when they stand and try to worship God publicly, it's a pure work of the flesh. They're just doing it because it's Sunday. There's no anointing on it. But when someone is a private worshipper, it overflows in public ministry. Something about them rubs off on you, because it's real in their own life.

'Neglect Not the Gift'

Paul says, "Be consumed with the gift that is in you." Notice what he says next in verse 14. If Timothy had been there, Timothy probably would have slapped his face for making this statement: "Neglect not the gift which is in thee, which was given thee by prophecy, with the laying on of the hands of the presbytery."

In the Greek, this is a prohibition. You would translate it, "Stop neglecting the gift." This word "neglect" is the Greek word *amelei*. This word *amelei* (or "neglect") refers to someone who is lazy, unconcerned, or slothful.

Timothy thought that was the last thing he was! He was working hard! In fact, he was trying to do everything. He was pouring himself out into the church. That's why he wrote Paul. He said, "Man, I'm working so hard, I've got to have some help." And Paul writes back in verse 14, "Now, stop being lazy."

"What? I'm not lazy!"

"Don't be slothful."

"What?"

"Stop being unconcerned and uncaring."

Timothy thought to himself, "What? When he knows all I'm doing, how in the world could he ever think I was unconcerned, uncaring, slothful, or lazy? I am pouring my life out. Everyone knows that."

Why does Paul call Timothy neglectful? Because the gift of God is so big on the inside of you, it doesn't matter how much you're doing; that gift wants to do *more*. And when we really have a revelation of how big the gift of Christ is on the inside of us, and we look at the way we're yielding to it, it doesn't matter if we're working with all our heart, or if we're yielded more than anyone else — we are still unconcerned, lazy, and uncaring in comparison to what that gift can become!

But, you see, there's a mentality in us that says, "I've done more than anyone else. I've set the example." There is no such thing as being a perfect example in this matter, and that is what Paul is saying to Timothy: "You haven't yielded like you can yield. The gift is bigger than you've ever imagined."

Notice what he says in verse 14: "Stop neglecting the *gift* that is in thee." This word "gift" is the Greek word *charisma*. This word *charisma* refers to something that is given by grace.

Supernatural Endowments

I think one reason why we neglect the gift that is in us is because we don't realize it is a supernatural endowment. It *is* a supernatural endowment.

There are times when we look at preaching like it is just another sermon. We forget that preaching is a supernatural endowment. Then there are those who have a music gift, and exhortation flows through them. In fact, it flows through them so often, they sometimes forget it was given to them supernaturally.

You can be so accustomed to the gifts of the Spirit that you no longer appreciate them. We need to remember these are not natural talents. These are not natural abilities. Paul says, "Neglect not the *charisma*, that which was given to you by grace." It is a supernatural endowment.

That gift inside you is not something you got from your piano teacher. It's not something you got because you sang in the junior high choir, the high school choir, and the church choir. It is a supernatural endowment given to you by God. And even when you use it every day of the year, you should recognize that it is a supernatural gift.

That is why, when I teach and feel a strong anointing, if someone comes to me afterwards and says, "Boy, that was good," I say, "By golly, it was great!" It sounds a little arrogant, doesn't it? But it's not arrogant. I know it's the gift in operation!

It's not me. I know who I am. And I'm not what comes out of me! It's a *charisma*. It's a grace-given gift. And do you know what? I am so aware that it's a gift that no one enjoys it more than I do!

Don't Lose Your Vision

"Neglect not the gift that is in thee, which was given thee by prophecy." Really, the Greek would be translated, "It was accompanied with prophecy." What does prophecy do? Prophecy reveals future events.

In First Timothy 1:18, Paul says, "This charge I commit unto thee, son Timothy, according to the" — what? — "prophecies which went before on thee, that thou by them mightest war a good warfare."

What Paul is really saying here is, "When God first called you, He also gave you a prophecy. He showed you what your ministry would accomplish. He showed you where your ministry was going to take you. He showed you how you were going to affect the world."

And Paul is saying to Timothy, "Have you fulfilled the call? If you have not yet completely fulfilled your call, then you can still yield to the gift, because the gift has more work to do."

When you were first called by God, can you remember the vision or the dream that God gave you along with that call? I remember vividly when the Lord called me into the ministry. I remember the vision. I had an open vision.

God showed me what I would be doing. And as long as that vision burns in my mind, I know that I still have a way to go, because I have not yet fulfilled what God showed me I would do.

That is why Paul said to Timothy, "You haven't done all that God told you to do. Why are you being unconcerned? You can still yield to that gift in a bigger way." So he says,

"Remember the prophecy which was given thee, with the laying on of hands of the presbytery."

Now look at verse 15. He says, "Meditate upon these things. The word "meditate" is the Greek word *meletao*. This word *meletao* means "take care of." You could translate it, "Think about these things." The best translation is the word "cultivate." "Cultivate these things." Or you could translate it, "Take special time to care and develop these things."

Again, we're talking about a devotion to development. Your preaching, teaching gift must be *cultivated*.

"Meditate upon these things; give thyself wholly to them." Especially notice the phrase, "give thyself wholly to them." This phrase is from the Greek word *isthi*, which means "live in them."

Be Up to Your Ears in Ministry!

Live and move and have your being in this call. Be consumed by these things. Be completely immersed in them. A secular piece of literature from the first century uses the same word, and there it is translated, "Be up to your ears in this."

The idea is, just like the body is surrounded by air, so your life should be surrounded by that call God placed on you. You should be in it, consumed with it, up to your ears in it. It should be your life.

". . .that thy profiting may appear to all." This word "profiting" means to make an advance. It is the word *prokope*, "to make an advance," or "to make progress." In one place it is translated "blaze the trail."

Why is it important for your profiting to appear to all? Because you're blazing the trail for the rest of the church. They will do what they see you do. And if they see you moving forward in the gifts of the Holy Ghost, it's going to help your church become more open. You are the one who will blaze the trail. But if you don't blaze the trail, no one's going to follow. So I would translate it, "Blaze the trail, that thy profiting may appear to all."

In verse 16, Paul continues, "Take heed unto thyself, and unto the doctrine; continue in them: for in doing this thou shalt save thyself, and them that hear thee."

Mark that phrase "Take heed unto thyself." This is the Greek word *epecho*. This word *epecho* I would translate, "Grab hold of yourself." Again, it's laying the responsibility on Timothy.

If these things are going to be cultivated in his life, then he must grab hold of himself. Paul says, "Timothy, grab yourself. Timothy, get hold of yourself. Timothy, you've got to turn your attention to yourself. You've got to get your life together in these things."

Laying the Proper Foundation

Now notice what Paul says next: "...and unto the doctrine." Notice again that Paul mentions *doctrine*. I want to tell you: The day of doctrine will never be over! I cannot imagine anyone thinking or teaching that the day of doctrine is over. Someone has said, "Well, this has been the day of teaching. There's good teaching everywhere. Now we can move beyond the Bible!"

You can't give enough foundation to the Church. As long as babies are being born, they're going to need foundation. Do you want to be a good minister? We saw that verse 6 of this chapter says, "Build a good foundation under your church, and you'll be a good minister of Jesus Christ."

God is very interested in foundation-laying. Yes, we've got to move beyond foundation; but, saints, we've always got to come back to it. It is the basis for everything else, and where there is no foundation, the structure is going to fall.

What I want you to see from this text is the devotion to development is on whose shoulders? It's on *our* shoulders. God has given us the *charisma* (gift), and we must yield to it. We must exercise ourself according to it.

I like the way Paul says it. He says, "We work according to the power that worketh in us." It's working in you. If you will work with it, you're going to get blessed.

A good minister of Jesus Christ always concerns himself with foundation. According to verse 6, God calls this minister good and delightful. As we seek to move on with God, let us never forget that God *loves* the foundation of His Word in our lives. It is the responsibility of the fivefold ministry gifts to get under the Church and put that solid foundation in place.

The next chapter will help you recognize true and false revelations. In a day when the New Age Movement and strange new teachings in the Church are springing up all around us, we need to have a measure or test to see which of these teachings and manifestations are of God. The Word is the measure one must use.

Rick Renner's Expanded Translation
of 1 Timothy 4:6-16
(Freely Translated)

If you spend your time and energies building a solid foundation underneath the brethren, you indeed will be the kind of minister in whom Jesus Christ finds great delight. Just like Jesus, you must consider yourself a slave and a servant. Building a foundation underneath people is hard, laborious work, yet it is this type of dedication that pleases God and makes you like Jesus, for He, too, came as a servant. In order to maintain this servant mentality, you must listen, receive, digest, and incorporate into your life the words of faith and good, excellent teaching. This is good news for you, Timothy, because you already have been following after these. You have a very good start.

You must absolutely reject with indignation and intolerance old wives' fables. Consider the old women's advice as good for nothing. Throw it out and treat it as manure. It has no place in the life of a real servant. Instead of taking their advice to take it easy, strip off every unnecessary weight in your life. As an athlete exercises hard while naked, take off those spiritual encumbrances and do everything within your power to develop spiritually. Make your devotion deep, committed, and determined. You must have a devotion to development.

Just as bodily exercise is good for your short-lived body, spiritual exercise and a deep devotion to development is profitable in all of your life now, and it lasts beyond this life, reaching into the life that is to come. What a promise!

This that I have just written to you is a faithful saying. Timothy, this isn't just a statement I'm making personally to you. Everyone should have this philosophy. It is worthy of all acceptation.

Because exercise causes further spiritual development, we are not afraid of the hardest work and do not despise agonizing situations. These difficult, laborious, strenuous, agonizing periods are making us more fit spiritually. This is the way we view life, putting all of our trust in the living God, who is the Savior of all men; especially of those that believe.

Timothy, these things I've said to you, you must say to others. You must transmit this teaching and bold way of living to your people. In fact, you should teach it, teach it, teach it, and teach it to them continuously. They can never hear this enough!

Let no man look down on you and judge you became you are young; this is not a time to succumb to their opinions of you. Rather, show them who you are! Don't back down. Start developing yourself. Start changing. This is an opportunity for exercise; especially develop in these areas: in word, in character, in love, in spirit, and in sexual purity. Make sure even your mind is morally clean. In these six areas you should become a type and example worthy of imitation.

Till I come, you must continue consistently and habitually giving yourself to the reading of scripture — not for the sake of a sermon, but for the sake of your own personal growth. This growth should first be reflected by deep spiritual fellowship around the Word with your closest friends. Then, finally, this growth will be reflected as you minister God's Word publicly. Your public ministry, however, should be an overflow from these other areas of your life. Public ministry is a result of personal growth.

Do not continue neglecting and ignoring the gift in your life. It is a supernatural endowment, full of power and ability. Regardless of how much you've already done, the gift in you is so powerful, it can do more. When God gave it to you, He also gave you a prophecy as the elders laid hands on you. God told you specifically what He would do through your ministry. Have you fulfilled all that prophecy? Then you must start yielding to the gift in a greater way. You have a mission to fulfill.

Take special time and care to cultivate these things. They will not develop by accident. You must decide to develop them. Give yourself to them completely. Be consumed with them, given to them, and almost driven until you feel you are up to your ears in them. Then you will really begin to grow. You will begin to forge new frontiers, and everyone will see your growth and be encouraged to follow.

Understand that your personal development is the first priority in your life. Grab hold of yourself and determine to cultivate growth in your life, and grab hold firmly onto doctrine. In fact, you must stay right by the Word and make it your number one business; for in doing this, you will personally experience a new measure of salvation and deliverance, and them that hear you preach and teach will be changed, too.

Chapter 8
How To Test Spiritual Manifestations

A very distraught person recently came to me and asked, "Should we test some of these new spiritual manifestations?" He continued, "When I began to think some of them through, they didn't line up with scripture. However, when I tried to bring it to the attention of the leadership, they said I was in the flesh and unspiritual for questioning certain teachings and new manifestations."

Yes, absolutely! New teachings, revelations, and spiritual manifestations should be tested. Especially in a day when the New Age Movement is growing so fast, and when strange new teachings — never before heard — are developing in the Church.

Remember, in First Timothy 4:1 the Holy Spirit emphatically said seducing spirits and doctrines of demons would attempt to invade the Church in the last days. We must be aware of these things and have a keen sense of responsibility — knowing that God will hold us accountable for what we teach and share with others.

Unfortunately, many have tried to tell us it is carnal or unspiritual to test new words from the Lord. Quite the contrary! When you test the spirits, this *does not* mean that you are opposing God or walking in unbelief. If the dream, vision, or new teaching is really from God, it *will* pass the test. Second, God will commend you for wanting to know the truth.

In the next two chapters we are going to learn how to test new spiritual manifestations. There are many examples of this type of testing in the Word of God. We will specifically look at the commendation Jesus gave the Ephesian Church for applying such a test to new ministries in their midst.

As you will see, Jesus never once condemned the Ephesian Church for asking questions, or for diligent research regarding a new teaching. Instead, He *commended them* for this type of intense, thorough examination of ministries, teachings, manifestations, and new doctrines. The church of Ephesus was highly developed in the way they tested new spiritual manifestations. They were the most sophisticated doctrinal examiners of their day.

First, however, let me give you an illustration of a dream that should have been tested. I was in a meeting and a woman came up to me and said, "May I have a few minutes to share a dream with you that the Lord gave me?"

I thought, "Well, if it was a dream from the Lord, I'm sure that it would be a blessing in my life." I said, "Sure, go ahead and tell me the dream," so she began to share the dream with me.

In the dream she said she went into a morgue and saw her family members lying there dead: her mother, her daddy, her brother, her sister, and her husband. She reached out and touched them. She said she tried to pick up their hands, but their hands were stiff. Rigor mortis had already set in.

She stood there in the dream and looked over to one side of the room and saw a chain saw on a chair. So she picked the chain saw up, pulled the cord, and the chain saw started. She walked over and began to give "autopsies" to all those corpses.

As she went on recounting this dream, I honestly thought I was going to get sick just listening to her. She said that once she looked inside the corpses, she began to cut them into pieces. She said, "What a bloody mess this dream was! I'd cut an arm off, and I'd cut a leg off."

Then she said, "Here's the interpretation: My family members are dead in sin. Rigor mortis has set in. They're dead in their sins, and they're dead in their rebellion, and God is going to raise me up to whack them into pieces. I am going to open their heart and look on the inside, almost like an autopsy, to see what it is that's causing them to be so rebellious against God. And if they do not repent, I will be used of God to bring destruction into their lives."

I said, "Well, what has this dream produced in your life?"

She answered, "Well, to be honest, I'm kind of happy about it. I feel a little vindictive about my relatives. I'm kind of happy about it."

A Demon-Inspired Dream

As I listened to this dream, she failed on every point on how to test a dream, vision, or angelic visitation. This was not a dream from the Lord. In fact, it sounded to me like a demon-inspired dream! That dream should have been tested.

We need to see specifically in scripture that there is a basis for testing these things. In First John chapter 4 verse 1, John says, "Beloved, believe not every spirit, but try the spirits...."

The word "try" could be translated "test." "But try [or test] the spirits, whether they are of God: because many false prophets are gone out into the world."

When you study the Ephesian Church in Revelation chapter 2, you discover they were judged by the Lord for having left their first love, but there was one thing they did for which the Lord commended them. He commended them for testing the spirits.

Revelation 2:2 says this: "I know thy works, and thy labour, and thy patience, and how thou canst not bear them which are evil: and thou hast tried them which say they are apostles, and are not, and hast found them liars."

Verse 3 continues, "And hast borne, and hast patience, and for my name's sake hast laboured, and hast not fainted."

The Church Jesus Visited

In verse 2, the Lord says to the Ephesian Church, "I know thy works...." This word "know" is the Greek word *oida*, which always refers to first-hand experience. Jesus apparently had paid many visits to the Ephesian Church. What He is about to describe was not related to Him by an angel, or through prayer.

Jesus had been inside the walls of this church — He had attended their church services, watched their worship, examined their zeal, and knew all about them. This, of course, is in agreement with chapter 2 verse 1, which tells us clearly that Jesus does walk in the midst of the seven golden candlesticks.

After walking in their midst and making a full examination of all their activities, He said, "I know your works. I've been there in your church and I've seen all you are doing. I know all of your activities."

Then the Lord began mentioning what He had discovered. He said, "I know thy works, and *thy labour*." The word "labour" is the Greek word *kopos*, which refers to exhaustive labor that results in weariness. This is the hardest type of toil and labor possible. It could be translated, "I know thy works, and I know the exhaustive labor which has resulted in causing you to be weary."

And then notice His next statement: "And I know *thy patience*." The word "patience" is the Greek word *hupomeno*. This is a compound of two Greek words, *hupo* and *meno*. *Hupo* means underneath, or under. The word *meno* is the Greek word which literally means, "I stay," or "I abide."

When the two words are compounded together, it means, "I am under an extremely heavy load, but have resolved not to move." Regardless of how heavy the load becomes, this person or church is not moving!

Ephesus: Crossroads for Controversy

What load were they under? "I know thy works, and thy labour, and thy patience, *and how thou canst not bear them which are evil....*" The Ephesian Church was on the road that linked the west to the east. Everyone traveled on that road. The Ephesian Church was one of the most famous churches of the first century. So everyone somehow or another seemed to make their way to Ephesus with a wonderful, new, dynamic revelation.

The Ephesian Church was a well-educated church when it came to the subject of scripture and doctrine. They knew what was right, and they knew what was wrong.

When you study Ephesians chapter 1, you find the Apostle Paul very quickly mentions predestination. He mentions election. He mentions foreknowledge. He mentions these lofty, lofty theological ideas and never even stops to teach on them. The reason he doesn't is because the Ephesian Church is already educated when it comes to these types of theological terms.

So what you find is, this powerfully educated church had no tolerance for error and refused to endorse false doctrine and silliness. They just wouldn't tolerate it. Flaky doctrine is something they would not permit in their church.

Now look again at what it says in verse 2: "I know thy works, and thy labour, and thy patience, *and how thou canst not bear them....*" The phrase "canst not" and the word "bear" are extremely important.

"Canst not" is the Greek word which means, "You do not have the power." Today we could translate it, "You have no tolerance." The word "bear" is the Greek word *bastadzo*, which means "to take or to bear responsibility for someone or something."

There are several good examples of this word in scripture. In John 10:31, Jesus is about to be stoned, and this word *bastadzo* is used. It says, "Then the Jews *took up* stones again to stone him." The two words "took up" is the same word "bear" (*bastadzo*) used in Revelation 2:2.

127

Another example is found in John 12:6. The Word says this, speaking of Judas Iscariot: "This he said, not that he cared for the poor; but because he was a thief, and had the bag, and *bare* what was put therein." This, too, is the Greek word *bastadzo*, which means Judas actually *had the money in his control, or he had it in his responsibility.* It was his responsibility. He was answerable for that which was in his care.

No Heretics Allowed

So when Jesus says, "and how thou canst not bear," He's describing an intolerable situation. And the word "bear" indicates, "We will not take responsibility for these types of people. We won't place our seal of approval on their doctrine, either. We will neither touch them, nor have anything to do with their irresponsible teachings."

"And thou hast tried them which say they are apostles, and are not, and hast found them liars." Notice particularly the Lord says, "and thou hast *tried* them." The word "tried" is the Greek word *peiradzo*, which means "to try," or "to test." It always refers to an examination of the most intense kind.

The indication here is that there was a high tribunal in the Church of Ephesus, and when a new doctrine was coming forth, or when someone claimed to be an apostle, this person would be interrogated. They were going to make sure the doctrine in their church was spotless, and that this strange, new doctrine would not make its way into the mainstream of the church.

So the Ephesians actually tried those who said they were apostles and were not, and they found many of them liars. The word "found" is the Greek word *eureka*, which means, "I found it."

It's almost as though Jesus says, "After hours and hours of examination, and careful consideration, the error surfaced! You knew in your spirit something was off track — and because of your patience and great care, it finally came out.

The mask of spirituality was removed, and you discovered them to be liars. *Eureka!"*

The Ephesians' conclusion was that these people were liars. The Greek word *pseudo* ("liar") speaks of a blatant, baldfaced liar. Notice, too, that they were not afraid to call the shots as they saw them. If they found you to be a liar, they labeled you and let your lying activities be known!

A Commendation for Patience

In Revelation 2:3, the Lord commends them for this type of doctrinal examination. He says, "And hast borne, and hast patience, and for my name's sake hast laboured, and hast not fainted." The Lord is commending them for wanting to maintain doctrinal purity.

The phrase "and hast" tells us about a *continuing action.* This not something they did only in earlier years; this is something they are *continuing to do all the time.* You could read it, "And hast *continually* borne."

The word "borne" is again the Greek word *bastadzo,* which was used back in verse 2, when the Lord said, "thou canst not *bear."* This word "bear" is translated "borne." Again, it refers to responsibility.

The Lord is saying, "You have borne continuous responsibility and have acted wisely. While you didn't put your stamp of approval on these liars, you did bear well your responsibility to maintain doctrinal purity." Then Jesus said, "and for my name's sake...hast not *fainted."* The word "fainted" means "to slowly grow weary from extra labor and strenuous action."

So the Lord commends them for wanting to maintain doctrinal purity and He says that their testing of pseudo apostles is really a very good idea. From the word of Jesus to the Ephesian Church, we see the Lord views the testing of new revelation as responsible action.

The Problem of False Apostles

In Second Corinthians chapter 11 we find another reason why it is important to test dreams, visions, angelic visitations, and new revelations. Paul says this in Second Corinthians 11: "For such are false apostles, deceitful workers, transforming themselves into the apostles of Christ. And no marvel; for Satan himself is transformed into an angel of light. Therefore it is no great thing if his ministers also be transformed as the ministers of righteousness. . ." (vv. 13-15).

This phrase "false apostles" is a Greek compound word, the word *pseudo*, which means "false," or "liar," and the word *apostolos*, which is the word for an apostle. When you put the two words together, it means "pseudo apostles." Paul says there are such things as lying apostles, or pseudo apostles. Then he describes them, calling them "deceitful workers."

The word "deceitful" is important. It is the Greek word *dolios*. *Dolios* is a word which refers to cunning, craftiness, trickery, or to someone who is treacherous. And in the very oldest sense, this word "deceitful" was used to describe a fisherman. Why? Because he used bait to catch fish.

By using the word *dolios*, Paul says that these pseudo apostles are baiting you! They're trying to draw you out for the bait, and their intention is that you might bite their false message and get hooked. A hook of deception, set in your jaw, would make it difficult for you to break free and get away from them.

Now notice the kind of intensity these false apostles possess. It says they are "deceitful workers." The word "workers" is a special clue to the great intensity with which they work. This is the Greek word *ergates*, which means they are hard at work.

They're not just hoping that the "fish" — in this case, believers — will bite; they are actually planning methods whereby the "fish" might be lured out, attracted, tempted, and led to take a bite. This describes "lying apostles" who are doing all they can to bait the saints and catch them with trickery.

Now notice what Paul says: "For such are false apostles, deceitful hard workers, transforming themselves into the apostles of Christ." That word "transforming" is an amazing word. It's from the Greek word *schema*. It refers to the *outward appearance*. It's the same word used in Philippians 2:8 to describe the incarnation of Jesus.

Philippians 2:8 says, "And being found in *fashion* as a man, he [Jesus] humbled himself, and became obedient unto death, even the death of the cross."

That same root is found here. It is the Greek word *schema*, which means "to change outwardly." The very oldest example we have of this word is of a king who traded his royal robes for sackcloth and ashes. His *outward appearance* changed.

Second Corinthians chapter 11 tells us these pseudo apostles transformed themselves into the apostles of Christ — they assumed a new, *outward appearance*. They were able to transform themselves so that they looked like the apostles of Christ.

You say, "Wow!" In verse 14, Paul says, "And no marvel." The word "marvel" is the Greek word for a "wonder." "And no *wonder!*" Paul continues. "Don't be shocked about this! For Satan himself is transformed into an angel of light." The word "light" is the Greek word *photos*, which refers to a brilliant, brilliant light.

What Leads People Into Deception?

The primary thing that leads people into deception is a desire for superior revelation. In New Testament times, a group called the Gnostics was invading the Church. The word *Gnostic* means "to know." They claimed superior knowledge, special revelation, or new light beyond anyone else — including Paul himself. They were misleading and beguiling many people away into false doctrine.

Today the New Age Movement is claiming to bring light to the world. They even talk about "the Christ," but they're not talking about the same Christ that we know. They're talking about a "Christ spirit" that has nothing to do with Jesus at all. And if you will plug into this "Christ spirit" in the universe, they say, it will bring light and revelation into your life.

Satan is no longer disguising himself as a devil with a pitchfork. Today he is coming to the world in the form of light. And Paul says, "And no marvel; for Satan himself is transformed into an angel of light."

Satan is a master at disguise! *The following three texts have establish the fact that we need to test spiritual manifestations and new teachings.* Our scriptural basis is: First John 4:1; Revelation 2:2,3; and Second Corinthians 11:13,14.

First John 4:1 tells us to test spirits. In Revelation 2:2,3, the Ephesian Church is *commended* for doing it. And in Second Corinthians 11:13,14, Paul says, "Don't be shocked! No marvel; for Satan himself is transformed into an angel of light."

When you test a dream, a vision, an angelic visitation, or a new revelation, this does not mean that you are opposing God or walking in unbelief. If your dream, vision, angelic visitation, or new revelation is from God, first of all, it will pass the test. And, second, God will commend you for your integrity in wanting to know the truth.

How To Test Your Revelation

When you test new teachings and spiritual manifestations, there are primarily *five questions* which you must ask.

1. *How did you receive it?*

2. *What is the content?* (This is an extremely important question.)

3. *Does it line up with the Word?*

4. *What does it produce in your life?*

5. *Whom does it glorify?*

We are going to be dealing with each of these five questions separately.

1. *How did you receive it?*

There are only two answers possible here. It either came from God or from Satan. However, there are many ways you find believers receiving revelation in scripture. Some are received through dreams, visions, and prayer. God's primary vehicle of revelation, however, is through *the Word*.

In Acts 9, we find that the Apostle Paul received his visitation from Jesus as he was slain in the Spirit: "And as he journeyed, he came near Damascus: and suddenly there shined round about him a light from heaven: And he fell to the earth, and heard a voice saying unto him, Saul, Saul, why persecutest thou me?" (vv. 3,4).

In Acts 26, where Paul elaborates even more when he is testifying before King Agrippa, he says, "Not only did I fall, but we all fell." In Acts 26, beginning in verse 13, Paul says this: "At midday, O king, I saw in the way [or in the road] a light from heaven, above the brightness of the sun, shining round about me and them which journeyed with me. And when we were all fallen to the earth, I heard a voice speaking unto me..." (vv. 13,14).

But notice in verse 14, "when we were *all* fallen to the earth." What you discover is, the Apostle Paul (then called Saul) and his companions are all knocked down and slain in the Spirit!

Frequently in the Old and New Testaments, you find that dreams, visions, angelic visitations, or new revelations happen when people are slain in the Spirit. Often dreams, visions, angelic visitations, or new revelations come while people are praying with other tongues. At other times you find that these things happen when people are simply quiet in the presence of the Lord.

When God Invades Your World

I want you to notice that while in prayer, being slain in the Spirit, praying in tongues, or being quiet, the recipient is not *seeking* a vision or a revelation. Rather, it is God seeking to break through into your world to give you the enlightenment or direction you need. It's God coming after you.

Again, this is contrary to the occult. People in the occult seek to make contact with the spirit realm. They are the initiators. But when God makes contact, *He is the Initiator.*

When a dream, vision, or angelic visitation took place in the Bible, it usually took the recipient by surprise. It was totally unexpected. The people involved were not initiating the contact; rather, God initiated it. They were simply in the right spiritual place to receive it. And the new revelation was always in agreement with the already revealed WORD OF GOD!

An example of this is found in Acts 9: "And there was a certain disciple at Damascus, named Ananias; and to him said the Lord in a vision, Ananias. And he said, Behold, *I am here, Lord.* And the Lord said unto him, Arise, and go into the street which is called Straight, and enquire in the house of Judas for one called Saul of Tarsus: for, behold, he prayeth, And hath seen in a vision a man named Ananias..." (vv. 10-12).

In prayer, Ananias heard from God.

In Acts 10, we find Cornelius had a vision while *in prayer:* "There was a certain man in Caesarea called Cornelius, a centurion of the band called the Italian band, A devout man, and one that feared God with all his house, which gave much alms to the people, and prayed to God alway" (vv. 1,2).

Verse 3 says, "He saw in a vision evidently about the ninth hour of the day...." Cornelius was *praying* when God revealed Himself to Cornelius. So we see two instances of revelation received *in prayer.*

Another instance of a revelation is found in Acts 10:9. It happened while Peter was praying: "On the morrow, as they went on their journey, and drew nigh unto the city,

Peter went up upon the housetop to pray about the sixth hour." So this next instance came about while Peter was *in prayer.*

> And he became very hungry, and would have eaten: but while they made ready, he fell into a trance,
>
> And saw heaven opened, and a certain vessel descending unto him, as it had been a great sheet knit at the four corners, and let down to the earth:
>
> Wherein were all manner of fourfooted beasts of the earth, and wild beasts, and creeping things, and fowls of the air.
>
> And there came a voice to him, Rise, Peter; kill, and eat.
>
> Acts 10:10-13

Notice verse 16 says, "This was done thrice." In other words, this was done three different times. Peter was about finished praying, and he was waiting on dinner. He wasn't expecting lightning bolts or earthquakes! He was just sitting quietly in the presence of the Lord, waiting for dinner! *God initiated the contact!*

Forbidden Ways To Receive Revelation

It is very important to know how you received this revelation. This is the reason why it is important to know: *There are forbidden ways to receive.*

The Word tells us how we are *not* to receive information about the future, and how we are *not* to make contact with the spirit realm, and I want us to look at these scriptures.

In Deuteronomy 18, God speaks specifically to the children of Israel about *forbidden* ways to receive from the spirit realm:

> When thou art come into the land which the Lord thy God giveth thee, thou shalt not learn to do after the abominations of those nations.
>
> There shall not be found among you any one that maketh his son or his daughter to pass through the fire,

or that useth divination, or an observer of times, or an
enchanter, or a witch.

Or a charmer, or a consulter with familiar spirits,
or a wizard, or a necromancer.

For all that do these things are an abomination
unto the Lord: and because of these abominations the
Lord thy God doth drive them out from before thee.

Thou shalt be perfect with the Lord thy God.

Deuteronomy 18:9:13

Notice in verse 13 that God required His people to be
perfect in this issue. "Don't mess up when it comes to this,"
the Lord is saying.

"There shall not be found among you any one that
maketh his son or his daughter to pass through the fire, or
that useth divination, or an observer of times, or an
enchanter, or a witch. Or a charmer, or a consulter with
familiar spirits, or a wizard, or a necromancer."

So there are ways that you are *not* to receive a dream,
vision, angelic visitation, or new revelation.

The Snake Gives It Away

One very famous psychic in the world today, claims to
have received her prophetic abilities from God. She
absolutely did not.

She uses crystal balls. She claims she sees into the
future. She is a prognosticator. She says the prophetic gift
she has was conferred upon her as a young woman, when
in the night, during the middle of a dream, a big, black
serpent crawled in bed with her, wrapped itself around her,
and imparted a prophetic gift to her. She fails the test. This
is no gift from God.

Right now all over the land there are people who claim
special knowledge and new light. Another well-known
psychic claims to have visions from God. They are not from
God. She fails the test on every point.

Yes, she *has* received visions. She *has* seen dreams. She
may have even seen angels. But they were *not* the angels

of God. She fails the test at every point. She uses crystals. She uses New Age technology. These things are not from God; they are forbidden by God.

So if a dream is received because you've been to a hypnotist, it's *not* from God. If a vision is received while you were with a fortuneteller, it's *not* from God. If you have received revelation about the future by a horoscope or from a charmer, or one who consults with familiar spirits, it's *not* from God.

The Ways God Speaks

There is only one way that God speaks supernaturally to His people, and that is by His Spirit — through prayer and through the Word of God.

Dreams, visions, an angelic visitation, being slain in the Spirit, praying with other tongues, being quiet in His presence are all various *forms* of prayer and THE WORD working in our lives.

Notice, it is never *us* attempting to gain a contact; rather, it is God breaking in on the privacy of our world to supply us with information we need. Normally these contacts from God will take us by surprise. *Our task is to be in a position to hear God's voice.* This is one major part of prayer, and a definite result of the Work working in our lives.

It is important to know how you received the dream, the vision, or the new revelation. God says there is no room for fortunetellers, crystal balls, horoscopes, or mediums. So if you received anything through these forbidden ways, you have already failed the test.

On the other hand, if you heard from the Lord through these other forms of prayer, or through THE WORD, you may pass the test. Know this: When God makes special contact with His people, the experience is always in agreement with THE WORD.

137

Strange, New Revelations

Now we come to the second question:

2. *What is the content?*

Two additional questions follow: (a) *Is it concrete with the Word?* and (b) *Is it some strange, new revelation?*

It is the tactic of the enemy to bring strange, new revelations. This is nothing new. The enemy wants to tell *you* that *you've* received something that no one else has ever heard before; that *you* know more than the pastor knows; that *you* know more than anyone else has ever known; and that this is an end-time revelation which has never been known by man before now, and *you have superior knowledge.* This is a very old tactic of the enemy.

The Word says in Genesis 3:

> Now the serpent was more subtil than any beast of the field which the Lord God had made. And he said unto the woman, Yea, hath God said, Ye shall not eat of every tree of the garden?
>
> And the woman said unto the serpent, We may eat of the fruit of the trees of the garden:
>
> But of the fruit of the tree which is in the midst of the garden, God hath said, Ye shall not eat of it, neither shall ye touch it, lest ye die.
>
> Genesis 3:1-3

Especially notice the phrase "neither shall ye *touch it,*" because this is the open door through which Satan came to deceive Eve. You say, "Well, why is it so important?" Because it reveals ignorance on the part of Eve.

Again, notice verse 3. Eve says, "But of the fruit of the tree which is in the midst of the garden, God hath said, Ye shall not eat of it, neither shall ye *touch it,* lest ye die." Her quote of God, "neither shall ye *touch it*" reveals ignorance.

Why? In Genesis 2:16,17, the Lord speaks concerning this tree: "And the Lord God commanded the man, saying, Of every tree of the garden thou mayest freely eat: But of the tree of the knowledge of good and evil, thou shalt not eat of it: for in the day that thou eatest thereof thou shalt surely die."

Notice again: ". . .thou shalt not eat of it: for in the day thou eatest thereof thou shalt surely die." *God never said a word about touching it — never!*

What you discover is, Eve had misunderstood God's instructions, or she was simply ignorant concerning the facts. Eve didn't understand the issue was obedience and disobedience. She thought there was actually something in the tree that was poisonous. She thought, "We shouldn't even get close enough to touch it, because the tree is poison."

Eve quotes God, "God hath said, Ye shall not eat of it, neither shall ye *touch it*, lest ye die." Notice verse 4: "And the serpent said unto the woman. . . ." Seeing Eve's ignorance, Satan moved in quickly to deceive her. He saw an open door through which he might enter to deceive her. Ignorance is always the basis for deception — always.

I'm thinking right now of a young man who was a member of my church. He was ignorant concerning the Word, but he wanted to be a real Bible scholar. He would not submit to authority. He decided that he could hear from God on his own, and he didn't need anyone else to help him.

He went straight to the Book of Revelation. What a dangerous place for a brand-new believer to begin! He began to study the Book of Revelation, and the devil began to prey on his ignorance. He began to dream up new revelations concerning the Book of Revelation.

How Pseudo Prophets Are Born

Recently I heard that this young man now believes he is *the beast* in the Book of Revelation. It began with ignorance. The enemy saw ignorance, and he slipped in to deceive. (Prior to his latest "revelation," this young man believed that he was one of the two end-time prophets.)

How about the little old lady who received this new revelation: The Holy Ghost and the Holy Spirit are two different persons because the *King James Version* uses both words!

Once I was in a meeting in California, and a man came up to me and said, "I am a prophet." I said, "Is that right?" He said, "Yes, I am one of the two *end-time* prophets." I said, "Why do you think this?" He said, "Because I had a vision." He was deceived.

The content of his vision was not concrete with the Word. And we must ask ourself: *Is it concrete with the Word, or is it some strange, new revelation?*

Look again in Genesis 3:3. "But of the fruit of the tree which is in the midst of the garden, God hath said, Ye shall not eat of it, neither shall ye *touch it,* lest ye die." This reveals ignorance.

"And the serpent said unto the woman, Ye shall not surely die: For God doth know that in the day ye eat thereof, then your eyes shall be opened. . . ." The serpent offered Eve, as he offers all of us, *superior knowledge; understanding beyond her wildest dreams.* He added, "Your eyes shall be opened, and ye shall be as gods, knowing good and evil" (v. 5).

Pay heed to that last phrase, ". . .ye shall be as gods, knowing good and evil." This is the greatest clue that Eve was totally ignorant concerning the Word of God. In reality, she and Adam already *were* as gods.

You'll say, "Explain!" *God doesn't know evil. All God knows is good.* The only "bad" God has ever experienced was in the person of Jesus Christ on the cross and during Jesus' three days in hell. Apart from that, God has never personally experienced evil. There is *no evil* in God. He is *only good.* (James 1:17,18.)

The Offer Eve Couldn't Refuse

So the serpent came and said, "What is wrong with you, Eve, is, you've never experienced evil. Take a bite of the fruit, and when you taste it, then you will be like God: You will know good and evil. You will be a *well-rounded* individual. Like God, you will know the Dark Side as well as the Bright Side."

This appealed to the *soul* of Eve, who didn't understand she was *already* like God. Because God only knows good. God does not know the Dark Side. This Dark, Evil Side attempted to come into heaven eons ago, and God cast it out, hurling Lucifer to a monumental destruction.

The following verses say, "And when the woman saw that the tree was good for food," — *it looked good* — "and that it was pleasant to the eyes," — *it was appealing* — "and a tree to be desired to make one wise," — *superior knowledge* — "she took of the fruit thereof, and did eat, and gave also unto her husband with her; and he did eat.

"And the eyes of them both were opened, and they knew that they were naked [or they *lost* their God-likeness and became *unlike* God]. . ." (vv. 6,7).

The Word Is the Last Word

The content of this new revelation was wrong. Although very appealing, it was not concrete with God's already revealed WORD. There is no such thing as a new revelation *superior* to the Word of God. There is no such thing!

The Word of God is the last word on any subject. And if you receive a prophecy, a dream, a vision, an angelic visitation, or a new revelation, it must always be in agreement with the Word. There will be no new, superior revelations better than the Word.

Chapter 9
Seducing Spirits and Doctrines of Demons

Remember our earlier text, ". . .giving heed to seducing spirits, and doctrines of devils" (1 Timothy 4:1)? You say, "Is it really possible for a believer to give heed to seducing spirits and doctrines of demons?" Absolutely. It happened all the time in the New Testament.

Most of Paul's epistles were written to correct doctrines of demons!

If you knew that it was a seducing spirit you were hearing, you wouldn't turn your head and listen to it, would you?

What Paul is saying here is: In the last days demons are going to become so seducing that people will not realize they are witnessing demonic activity. And the demons are going to begin to operate in such a tantalizing way that it will actually cause people to stop, look, and turn their head to listen and look in a different direction — rather than curse and rebuke the demons.

Turning from the faith and opening up their mind to new ideas and new revelations will be the first step to being deceived. Revelation that is so *new* that you can't find it in the Word is *not* from God. You can be sure of it!

A Cloak of Respectability

Often demons come to twist the truth. They come to manifest their own teachings, and sometimes they wrap them up in spiritual terms that sound *acceptable,* even to the Church. And what a tragedy it is! How often believers get caught up in teachings which really do not matter.

God is concerned about *the content* of supernatural manifestations and fresh revelations. This is important to Him.

I want you to look at another dream and vision — a revelation that was received as though from God, but it was *not* from God. Colossians 2:18 says this: "Let no man beguile you of your reward in a voluntary humility and worshipping of angels, intruding into those things which he hath not seen, vainly puffed up by his fleshly mind." Read that again.

Now verse 19: "And not holding the Head, from which all the body by joints and bands having nourishment ministered, and knit together, increaseth with the increase of God."

Look again at verse 18: ". . . intruding into those things which he hath not seen, vainly puffed up by his fleshly mind."

This is what had happened in the Colossian Church: The Gnostics were in Colosse. (Remember, the word "Gnostic" means "to know," and this word was used to describe those who claimed *superior knowledge.*) The Gnostics claimed to have revelation and knowledge that no one else had. In fact, they believed they had superior knowledge even above that possessed by the Apostle Paul.

The Gnostics' Doctrine of Devils

One of their revelations was this: God was a holy God, and the earth was an evil earth. And because God was holy and the earth was evil, the two should never meet.

So in order for God to come to the earth, God would have to go through a process of de-evolution. God would have to emit a lower form of God, and that form of God emitted yet another lower form of God, and that another lower, and that another lower, and that another, and another,

and another, and so forth, until finally the very lowest form
of God that could ever be created was created and was born
on the earth — and His Name was *Jesus.*

The Gnostics believed that Jesus was the very lowest
form of God. They believed there was almost no God in Him.
These Gnostics had a doctrine of devils!

They believed that Jesus was just the starting point.
Once you receive Jesus, they taught, then you have the
wonderful opportunity to meet the form of God above Him,
and then the form of God above that one, and then the form
of God above that one, and so forth.

They actually were intruding into things that they had
not seen: doctrines of demons, the worship of angels — *going
beyond Jesus,* trying to get to know forms of Deity better and
more powerful than Jesus.

This is why in verse 19 Paul says to them, "And not
holding the Head, from which all the body by joints and
bands having nourishment ministered, and knit together,
increaseth with the increase of God."

The Price of Fanaticism

In verse 18, he says, "This wrong revelation is going to
beguile you of your reward." False doctrines, or doctrines
of demons — things that come from the spirit realm, not
from the Spirit of God — will beguile you of your reward!
That's why *the content* of the revelation is extremely
important.

Now go over to Hebrews chapter 13. Again, the question
is: *What is the content?* Hebrews 13:9 says this: "Be not carried
about with divers and strange doctrines." Notice this
statement carefully. Specifically pay heed to the phrase
"carried about." It's the idea of being *carried* by these things,
of being *consumed* by these things, or of having a *fascination*
with these things.

And what you discover is this — and I'm sure you have
experienced this sometime in your own life — when you

have a strange doctrine, *it consumes you.* It's all that you can see. It's all that you want to talk about. And it's almost like you gain a strange fascination for these things.

The writer of Hebrews continues, "Be not carried about with divers and strange doctrines. For it is a good thing that the heart be established with grace; not with meats, which have not profited them that have been occupied therein" (Hebrews 13:9).

So what is the content? Is it concrete with the Word, or is it some strange, new revelation? Now that we've covered the first two questions, it's time to move to the third.

3. *Does it line up with the Word?*

A revelation should always line up with the Word of God. In fact, *God never does anything apart from His Word.* Even if the Holy Spirit speaks to you, He will confirm the Word.

The Holy Spirit gave you the New Birth, but First Peter chapter 1 verse 23 says that you are born again *by the Word of God.* The Holy Spirit planted *the Word* within you.

When the angel came to Mary, he came *quoting the Old Testament.*

When the angel came to Joseph, he came *quoting the Old Testament.*

When the angel came to the shepherds, he came *quoting the Old Testament.*

When the Holy Spirit speaks, He does not add to the Word. He *confirms* the Word.

'Seducers Shall Wax Worse And Worse'

In Second Timothy 3:13, the Word says: "But evil men and seducers shall wax worse and worse, deceiving, and being deceived."

The word "seducers" is the Greek word *goes,* which means "one who gives incantations," or "one who uses magic or sorcery." And notice what it says about occultist activity: "But evil men and seducers shall wax worse and worse."

Really, what the Word is teaching here is that, as the coming of the kingdom of God approaches — as the coming of Jesus approaches — those in the occult are going to become more proficient in their activities than they've ever been. Those who use sorcery, magic, and incantations shall wax worse and worse. And notice their intention: Their intention is to deceive: "deceiving and being deceived." They're going to be caught up in their own deception.

The Believer's Protection

Now look at Second Timothy 3:14,15 to see how we can be protected from this error. It says, "But continue thou in the things which thou hast learned and hast been assured of, knowing of whom thou hast learned them; And that from a child thou hast known the holy scriptures, which are able to make thee wise unto salvation through faith which is in Christ Jesus."

Notice the phrase "continue thou." It is the Greek word *meno*, which means "to abide, or to remain permanently." The Lord uses this word in John chapter 15 verse 4. I want you to see this. It is a very important statement: "Abide in me, and I in you. As the branch cannot bear fruit of itself, except it abide in the vine; no more can ye, except ye abide in me."

Then, in verse 7, Jesus says, "If ye abide in me, and my words abide in you, ye shall ask what ye will, and it shall be done unto you." In every one of these instances, the word "abide" is the same Greek word *meno*.

Verse 7 could be translated, "If ye *meno* in me, abide in me, and my words *meno* in you, abide in you...." Again, it means *to permanently abide:* "If you permanently abide in me, and my words permanently abide in you.... If you have found a permanent residency in me, and my words have found a permanent residency in you...." We're talking about *permanence.*

With this word *meno* in mind, look again at Second Timothy 3:14, where Paul uses this word *meno*. "But continue *permanently* in the things which thou hast learned." The word "learned" is the Greek word *manthano*, which means "to learn as a student." This would be the very word used to describe a child that enrolls in school and begins to learn.

Paul says, "Continue thou in the things that you learned as a student. . . ." — indicating that Timothy has studied these things with great diligence. Verse 15: "And that from a child thou hast known the holy scriptures." The Greek literally says, "the holy writings."

You've known them from beginning to end. You've studied all the holy scriptures, the holy writings "which are able to make thee wise unto salvation through faith which is in Christ Jesus."

The Power of the Word

Why do people listen to seducing spirits? Why do people turn their heads toward strange, new doctrines and revelations? Because they want superior wisdom. They want something no one else has. They want to be able to boast of something that no one else can boast of. We might say that they want extra-special wisdom.

Paul, speaking to Timothy, says, "If you want wisdom, stay in the Word." Paul says this again in verse 15: "And that from a child thou hast known the holy scriptures, which *are able. . . .*"

These two words, "are able," are from the Greek word *dunamis*, or "power." Paul says, "The scriptures have the power to make you wise." Real wisdom is in the Word — powerful, powerful wisdom! ·

And then Paul says this in verses 16 and 17: "All scripture is given by inspiration of God, and is profitable for doctrine, for reproof, for correction, for instruction in righteousness: That the man of God may be perfect, thoroughly furnished unto all good works."

In verse 16, specifically give attention to the word "inspiration." This word "inspiration" means that it is God breathed. It wasn't written by men who simply had a good idea. It was delivered *through* men who literally *received* the very breath of God into their spirit and into their soul. These were words of scripture that came right *out of* the very being of God.

The New Testament scriptures are not scriptures that tell us *about* God; they are scriptures that *came out of* God. And contained in scripture itself is *the* life of God. *There is an element of God contained in the Bible itself.* It is God-breathed. The breath of the supernatural is in the Word.

By using this word "inspiration," Paul is saying to Timothy, "It's the highest revelation." You will never receive a dream, vision, angelic visitation, or new revelation with more of God in it than the scriptures contain. *The scriptures are the highest form of revelation.*

The Profit of Scripture

So Paul says, "All scripture is given by inspiration of God." And notice what it will do for you: "and is profitable." This is the Greek word for "beneficial." It's going to do something good in your life. It is profitable "for doctrine, for *reproof.*"

The word "reproof" means "to prove something," or "to convict you of something." It is profitable for correction. The word "correction" means "to put you in line," or "to put things straight."

So if you have messed up your life, the Word of God itself has the power to set you straight! Verse 16 concludes, "for instruction in righteousness." The word "instruction" is the Greek word *paideuo*, which means "to be in school as a little child."

Really, the intention of this word *paideuo* is that you can move from one level to another. When you finish that level, you can be promoted to the next level. You can go as far as you want to when it comes to the revelation of God's Word. It's up to you how far you want to go. You can go a long, long way with the Word: one promotion, another promotion, another promotion, another promotion in the school of continuing education in the Word of God. Why would we ever need a revelation beyond the Bible? There is enough revelation here to keep us expanding and learning for all eternity.

Then, in verse 17, Paul says this is the reason: "That the man of God may be perfect, thoroughly furnished unto all good things." We all want to be perfect. The word "perfect" is the Greek word *artios*, which means "to be fit," or "to be complete."

It can be translated "to be capable," or "to be sufficient." It's referring to someone who has moved into a superior position in life. And it did not come through some strange, new revelation. Rather, this superior, fit, capable, sufficient position in life was imparted into you through the inspiration of God's Word in your life. This divine revelation (THE WORD) has power to mature and equip you!

'Thoroughly Furnished'

The scripture goes on to tell us what we'll be like when the Word is working in our lives! It says we will be "thoroughly furnished unto all good works." "Thoroughly furnished" in the Greek rendering would literally be "completely outfitted."

In ancient Greek, it's used to describe a boat. You could just buy a boat, or you could buy a boat that was "loaded" — that was completely outfitted — a boat that had all the special little trinkets and gadgets on it that sailors love.

What the Word is teaching here is, if you let God's Word work in your life — if you let the Word which you hold in your hands. . .that Word that contains God in it — work in your life, you will find that this Word will take you and change you from an average believer into a "loaded" believer — a believer who is thoroughly furnished in every way imaginable.

Verse 17 says "thoroughly furnished unto all good works." This means, the Word of God will equip you so you'll be able to handle anything in life. Any assignment that God should give you, you'll be able to do. You'll be completely furnished unto every good work.

Testing the Spirits

I want you to see that Paul makes comparisons in Second Timothy chapter 3. First of all, he discusses seducers. He says they're going to get worse and worse. He says that deception is going to get worse. Their power of seduction is going to get more powerful. Their seducing is going to become more involved, intricate, and complex. Strange, strange revelations will emerge.

Second, Paul says, "But you continue — continue thou in the things which thou hast learned." Your new insight, light, and special revelation must line up with God's Word. It must!

In the same way, in First John chapter 4, John asks some specific questions concerning new revelation. Verse 1 says this: "Beloved, believe not every spirit, but try [test] the spirits whether they are of God: because many false prophets are gone out into the world." And in verses 2 and 3, John basically asks, "Do these new teachings and supernatural encounters agree with scripture?"

Look at verses 2 and 3: "Hereby know ye the Spirit of God: Everyone that confesseth Jesus Christ is come in the flesh is of God: And every spirit that confesseth not that Jesus Christ is come in the flesh is not of God: and this is that spirit of antichrist, whereof ye have heard that it should come: and even now already is it in the world" (vv. 2,3). Our revelations must line up with the revelation of God's Word!

Confusion or Peace?

Now we come to the fourth question:

4. *What does it produce in your life?*

To thoroughly cover this question, we must see what the Word says in James 3:13. It says, "Who is a wise man and endued with knowledge among you?" A paraphrase would be: "Who is the man who believes that he has superior wisdom? Who is a man; a wise man?"

The word "wise" is the word *sophos,* which refers to wisdom. "Who is the man with wisdom and endued with knowledge?" This indicates special knowledge, endued, superior, *special knowledge.* The entire thirteenth verse reads, "Who is a wise man and endued with special knowledge among you? let him shew out of a good conversation [a good life] his works with meekness of wisdom."

Now look at verses 14 through 16: "But if ye have bitter envying and strife in your hearts, glory not, and lie not against the truth. This wisdom descendeth not from above, but is earthly, sensual, devilish. For where envying and strife is, there is confusion and every evil work."

The fourth question that we're dealing with is: *What does this new teaching or manifestation produce in your life?*

Let's look at verse 13 again: "Who is a wise man and endued with special knowledge among you? let him shew [or let him prove it] out of a good conversation [a good life] his works with meekness of wisdom."

Meekness and wisdom add credibility to a new revelation. But in verse 15, James says, "If this is not in your attitude, then your revelation may *not* be from above." Now look at verses 14 and 15: "But if ye have bitter envying and strife in your hearts, glory not, and lie not against the truth. This wisdom descendeth not from above, but is earthly, sensual, devilish."

False Revelation: Source of Strife

In verse 14, the phrase "bitter envying" is very important. It's the Greek word *zelos,* which refers to a *fierce desire to promote your own idea to the exclusion of others.* Then you find out that it's really even a step worse than that.

Verse 14: "But if ye have bitter envying and *strife*." The word "strife" is the Greek word *eritheia*, which means "rivalry," or "ambition." It also can be translated, "a party spirit," or "a divisive spirit."

We find this also in First Corinthians chapter 1. From this we discover you don't have to be a devil worshipper to have the doctrine of demons, or to be *misled*. We see in First Corinthians chapter 1 that *eritheia* (strife) was in the Corinthian Church:

> Now I beseech you, brethren, by the name of our Lord Jesus Christ, that ye all speak the same thing, and there be no divisions among you; but that ye be perfectly joined together in the same mind and in the same judgment.
>
> For it hath been declared unto me of you, my brethren, by them which are of the house of Chloe, that there are contentions [*eritheia* — rivalries] among you.
>
> Now this I say, that every one of you saith, I am of Paul; and I of Apollos; and I of Cephas; and I of Christ.
>
> Is Christ divided? was Paul crucified for you? or were ye baptized in the name of Paul?
>
> 1 Corinthians 1:10-13

Eritheia is translated "rivalry," but it can also be translated "ambition," and it was used to describe political parties. So it is a party spirit which says, "We're right and you're wrong."

Back in James 3:14, James says, "If ye have bitter envying," or, "if you have *a fierce desire to promote your own ideas* to the exclusion of others, if you are *in rivalry* about your revelation, if you're *full of ambition*, if you're actually developing *a party spirit* in the church, glory not, and lie not against the truth." He says, "You are caught in a deception."

In verse 15, James continues, "This wisdom descendeth not from above, but is *earthly. . . .*" *Epigeios* is the word in Greek which means it's from an earthly dimension. It does not come from heaven. Second, James says it is "sensual" *(psuchikos)*, which means "this is *soulish*, not spiritual." Third, James says, "It is devilish." The Greek word is *daimoniodes*, or the word "demons." Or, James says, "You are demonized."

People do not willingly become demonized. Demonization takes place very slowly — it, too, is a work of seducing spirits. Obviously a person would have to be deceived to believe they were correct by having a fierce desire to promote themselves to the exclusion of others. A person would have to be deceived to bring rivalry, ambition, and a party spirit into the church.

James says, "It is obvious this person's soul has come under the influence of demonic activity. The fruit of their new revelation doesn't line up with the fruit of the Spirit. Through sincere, these individuals are wrong and sorely demonized."

Now look at verse 16, where James says, "For where envying and strife is, there is *confusion* and every evil work." This Greek word "confusion" means "disorder, disturbance, trouble, and instability." This is not what God produces.

I would translate this verse, "For where envying and strife are, *there is disorder, disturbance, trouble, instability, and every evil work.*"

The word "evil" is the Greek word which means "something that is foul, wicked, or vile." So if a new revelation produces strife, bitterness, ambition, rivalry, party spirit, confusion, disorder, disturbance, trouble, or instability, it's *not* from God. And you'd better deal with it, because eventually *it's going to produce bad, foul, wicked, vile things in every part of your life.*

The Fruit of Righteousness

Then, in verse 17, James tells us *what God produces.* Let's look at this verse:

> But the wisdom that is from above is first pure, then peaceable, gentle, and easy to be intreated, full of mercy and good fruits, without partiality, and without hypocrisy.

Notice the words "pure," "peaceable," "gentle," and the phrase "easy to be intreated." James continues, "Full of mercy and good fruits, without partiality and without hypocrisy.

"And the fruit of righteousness is sown in peace of them that make peace" (v. 18).

Verse 17 begins, "But the wisdom that is from above is first pure...." The Greek word *agnos*, which means "pure," implies sincerity and integrity. It is spotless. It is pure.

Second, James says that it is *eirenikos* (peaceful), which means it is "peace-promoting." It's going to bring purity to the church. It's going to be peace-promoting.

Then he says that it is gentle. And the word "gentle" means "submissive"; even submissive to scrutiny. If your experience is really from God, you don't have to go on a rampage and tell everyone that it's from God, whether you agree with it or not. The wisdom that is from above is gentle. It is submissive, subject to scrutiny. It will pass the test of submission.

Then James says, "It is easy to be intreated." Take a note of this phrase "easy to be intreated." It means "easily persuaded," or "willing to yield, compliant." This Greek word is the opposite of the word "disobedient."

So we find that if a supernatural experience or teaching is really from heaven, it makes you more willing to yield. It makes you compliant. It makes you adaptable. It makes you to be easily persuaded, the opposite of disobedient. "Full of mercy and good fruits, without partiality, and without hypocrisy."

A wonderful translation of verse 17 would be: "But the wisdom that is from above is first and foremost pure; it is full of integrity and spot-free of impure motives. Second, real heavenly wisdom is peace-promoting; it will bring a wonderful sense of peacefulness and unity to those who hear it. Heavenly wisdom is gentle; it is so solid, so confident, and so full of God, that it will happily submit to scrutiny and examination — knowing that it will pass the test, if not now, then later — in time heavenly wisdom always comes to be recognized as true — therefore, it has no need to fight for itself; time will prove it true. This type of wisdom does not make a person uncontrollable, arrogant, and proud; rather, when God's wisdom works in you, it makes you more compliant to the needs of others. It is full of mercy and good fruits, without partiality, and without hypocrisy."

Verse 18 reads: "The fruit of righteousness is sown in peace of them that make peace." It could be translated two different ways. "The fruit of righteousness is sown by those who do peace," or even better, "The fruit of righteousness is for peaceable people."

But I want you to see very clearly: *What does it produce in your life?* Does it produce *confusion*, or does it produce *peace*?

Revelations Must Glorify Jesus

The last question is:

5. *Whom does it glorify?*

If it is from God, it *will* glorify Jesus. It will not glorify the angel; it will not glorify the dream; it will not glorify *you*. It will glorify *Jesus* if it is from God.

John 14:26 says this about revelation from the Spirit: "But the Comforter, which is the Holy Ghost, whom the Father will send in my name, he shall teach you all things, and bring all things to your remembrance, *whatsoever I have said unto you*." Jesus said this.

Then we see in John 15:26, "But when the Comforter is come, whom I will send unto you from the Father, even the Spirit of truth, which proceedeth from the Father, *he shall testify of me*." Jesus said this. So it glorifies Jesus.

John 16:13-15 says:

> **Howbeit when he, the Spirit of truth, is come, he will guide you into all truth: for *he shall not speak of himself*; but whatsoever he shall hear, that shall he speak: and he will shew you things to come.**

He shall *glorify me:* for he shall *receive of mine,* and shall *shew it unto you.*

All things that the Father hath are mine: therefore said I, that *he shall take of mine,* and shall *shew it unto you.*

Revelation 1:1 says this: "The Revelation of Jesus Christ, which God gave unto him, to shew unto his servants. . . ." The word "Revelation" is *apokalupsis,* which means "to part the veil and look beyond on the other side."

Notice the title of this book, according to Revelation 1:1. It is not the Revelation of things *to come.* What is it? It is *the Revelation of Jesus Christ.* Jesus is at the very heart of this Revelation.

Genuine Revelations Encourage You

So a God-given supernatural manifestation, experience or new revelation always glorifies Jesus — always! Somehow or other, it will encourage you to serve the Lord better. Martin Luther is a wonderful example of this.

While Luther did not receive a supernatural experience, the Word opened up to him in a way he had not previously known. There in the scripture, he saw — he received a *rhema* — a new understanding — a new revelation — that salvation was by faith, and not of works as he had been taught.

Although Luther did not actually have a visit with Jesus Himself, this new understanding drew him closer to Jesus. It caused his walk with the Lord to become a reality in his life, rather than a religious tradition. So powerful was this new revelation that it literally brought the world out of the Dark Ages into the Age of Enlightenment!

The end result of this revelation was a new understanding that everyone had available to him a life of faith. It glorified the work of Jesus Christ.

Polycarp, Bishop of Smyrna, is another wonderful and excellent example of how a supernatural encounter will somehow help you serve the Lord better.

Tradition says Polycarp had a dream one night in which he saw the pillow under his head burning with an intensely hot fire. Somehow Polycarp felt this was a warning from God. He sensed God was warning him of an imminent death by fire.

According to tradition, this revelation so prepared Polycarp for his death that when they came to take him, he willingly went with them — knowing that Jesus Christ would stand by him in the flame. He had absolutely no fear — and the multitudes watched as he stood true to the Person of Jesus Christ.

You say, "Well, he didn't see Jesus in that dream."

But that dream did give him the grace to serve Jesus better in the flame. You see, it produced something good in his life: Polycarp ended up glorifying God in his death! This dream helped him glorify Jesus Christ.

We've dealt with five questions, and they're all very important. Let's review these five questions.

1. *How did you receive it?* Did you receive it in prayer, or did you receive it from occult activity? Occult activity is forbidden by God.

2. *What is the content?* Is it concrete with the Word of God, or is it some strange, new revelation?

3. *Does it line up with the Word?* Does it line up with the inspiration of scripture according to Second Timothy 3:13-17? Does it tell us that Jesus Christ came in the flesh? Is it in agreement with scripture concerning Jesus?

4. *What does it produce in your life?* Confusion? (James 3:13-16.) If so, it's not from above. Peace? (James 3:17,18.) The wisdom from above is, first of all, pure, peaceable, gentle, full of mercy, without partiality.

5. *Whom does it glorify?* Does it glorify Jesus, or does it glorify a dream? Does it glorify the angel, or does it glorify the vision? Does it glorify *you*, or does it glorify Jesus? These are vitally important questions.

The Importance of Being Responsible

I want you to see again that the Lord is blessed when His people try to have integrity with new revelations and new teachings. The Lord does not hold it against you because you tested a vision that proved to be from Him. That test proves that you want truth, and it will pass the test if it's from God. That's not going to hurt God. God is going to be happy about your integrity.

In Revelation 2, Jesus said, "I know thy works, and thy labour, and thy patience, and how thou canst not tolerate [or bear responsibility for] them which are evil: and how thou hast tested them which say they are apostles, and are not, and hast found them liars: And hast borne responsibility in this respect, and hast patience, and for my name's sake hast laboured [for my name's sake; purity of doctrine], and hast not fainted" (vv. 2,3).

In First John 4:1, John said, "Beloved, believe not every spirit, but try [or test] the spirits whether they are of God: because many false prophets are gone out into the world."

God wants us to be responsible with spiritual manifestations. Today the world is full of supernatural manifestations, both from God and from Satan.

While we do not need to develop a fear about these things, we do need to deal wisely with new revelations. Satan desires to infiltrate the Church with error. He knows a real move of God is about to be loosed in the Church. The anointing that was on Moses is going to be released through us to confront the powers of the New Age.

During this crucial period of these last days, let us come before the cross, empty ourselves before the Lord, and yield to the strongest current of power the earth has ever seen!

This is a day of SEDUCING SPIRITS AND DOCTRINES OF DEMONS. We must have God's power to captivate the attention of the lost world! Only one thing now hinders this great move of power from flowing through the

Church — us! God needs only one thing — just one — He needs a channel!

Our prayer should be: "Make me a channel of blessing today. Make me a channel of blessing, I pray. Lord, channel your Word and your Spirit through us! Make us a channel!"

We conclude with the words of the Psalmist in Psalm 24:7-10:

> **Lift up your heads, O ye gates;** [Here we are called gates! *We* decide when this last move of God's power will begin! The door to this move is in our power! We are the gates!] **and be ye lifted up, ye everlasting doors;** [doors through which His power can flow — *we* are those doors!] **and the King of glory shall come in.** [He will pass His glory and majesty into the Church and world through *yielded vessels* — *that's us!*]
>
> **Who is the King of glory? The Lord strong and mighty, the Lord mighty in battle.** [And ready for a last day's battle and confrontation!]
>
> **Lift up your heads, O ye gates; even lift them up, ye everlasting doors; and the King of glory shall come in.**
>
> **Who is this King of glory? The Lord of hosts, he is the King.**

Let this great confrontation begin!

To order tapes by Rick Renner,
or to contact him for speaking engagements,
please write:

Rick Renner Ministries
P. O. Box 1709
Tulsa, Oklahoma 74101-9423

Books by Rick Renner

Dream Thieves
Dressed to Kill
Merchandising the Anointing
Living in the Combat Zone
Seducing Spirits and Doctrines of Demons
The Point of No Return
The Dynamic Duo
Spiritual Weapons to Defeat the Enemy